Ghost Stories of Canada

GHOST
STORIES
OF CANADA

JOHN ROBERT COLOMBO

with drawings by Jillian Hulme Gilliland

A HOUNSLOW BOOK
THE DUNDURN GROUP

TORONTO · OXFORD

Publisher: Anthony Hawke
Editor: Don McLeod
Design: Jessica Hexham
Printer: Webcom

Canadian Cataloguing in Publication Data

Colombo, John Robert, 1936-
    Ghost stories of Canada

ISBN 0-88882-222-7

1. Ghosts — Canada. I. Title.

BF1472.C3C64 2000   133.1'0971   C00-931772-4

ONTARIO ARTS
COUNCIL

THE CANADA COUNCIL | LE CONSEIL DES ARTS
FOR THE ARTS | DU CANADA
SINCE 1957 | DEPUIS 1957

Canada

CONSEIL DES ARTS
DE L'ONTARIO

We acknowledge the support of the **Canada Council for the Arts** and the **Ontario Arts Council** for our publishing program. We also acknowledge the financial support of the **Government of Canada** through the **Book Publishing Industry Development Program**, **The Association for the Export of Canadian Books**, and the **Government of Ontario** through the **Ontario Book Publishers Tax Credit** program.

Care has been taken to trace the ownership of copyright material used in this book. The author and the publisher welcome any information enabling them to rectify any references or credit in subsequent editions.

J. Kirk Howard, President

Printed and bound in Canada.⊕
Printed on recycled paper.

www.dundurn.com

Second Printing: November 2000

Dundurn Press
8 Market Street
Suite 200
Toronto, Ontario, Canada
M5E 1M6

Dundurn Press
73 Lime Walk
Headington, Oxford,
England
OX3 7AD

Dundurn Press
2250 Military Road
Tonawanda NY
U.S.A. 14150

Contents

Preface 11
Acknowledgements 17

Maritimes
The Fairy Companion 21
A Night with the Fairies 22
The Phantom Trapper 23
The Fire-Ship of Northumberland Strait 24
The Phantom Ship of the Bay of Chaleur 26
The Grey Lady of Annapolis Royal 27
The Teazer Light 28
The Battle in the Sky 28
The Ghost of Dr. Copeland's Wife 30
The *Fairie Queene* 31
The *Charles Haskell* 32
Mr. Extry Man 33
Joshua Slocum's Ghost 35
The Codfish Man 36
The Colonel's Ghost 37
The Wynyard Apparition 38
The Great Amherst Mystery 40
The Fire-Spook of Caledonia Mills 43
The Little Man Who Wasn't There 46
The Phantom Train of Bras d'Or 47
Haliburton House 48
Hopper's Headstone 48
The Dungarvon Whooper 49
"52 North by 21 West" 50
The Female Phantom of Gagetown 52
Christ Church Ghost 53
The Rowing Man 54
Vision of a Newly Dead Friend 54
The Little Man 55
The Prophet's Room 56
The UPEI Haunting 57

Quebec

The Talking Head	63
The Quebec Werewolf	64
The Hudson Poltergeist	64
Another Hudson Poltergeist	65
The Walling-in of Peggy Green	68
The Dagg Poltergeist	69
Dr. Brunelle's Crisis Apparition	71
A Singular Case	72
Stalked by a Ghost	73
The Haunting of Willow Place Inn	75
La Vieille Chapelle Ramsay	75

Ontario

The Baldoon Mystery	81
Old McAfee	83
The Eldon House Ghost	84
Welsh Lullabies	84
Tom Thomson's Ghost	85
The Vision of Old Walt	87
Ambrose Small, Missing Man	89
An Early Morning Visitor	91
The Ghost of St. Columbkill's	92
The Vision of the Chapel	93
Mackenzie King's Ghost	94
The Haunting of Mackenzie House	103
The Haunted Bookshop	108
Elizabeth the Ghost	109
The Haunting of Glanmore	110
The Screaming Tunnel	112
The Bilotti House	113
The Beautiful Lady in White	115
The Ghost of the Alex	116
The Gibson-Atwood Ghost	118
A Very Strange Experience	120
The Sticky Man	122
The Vision of a Crime	124
"Betty Louty"	127

Apparition of a Cat   129
Hunting Henry's Ghost   131
The Most Beautiful Woman in the World   135
Short Circuit   137

Prairies
The White Horse   143
Spirit of White Eagle   144
Who Calls?   145
The Vanishing Village   145
Frog Lake Vision   147
The Travelling Ghost   148
The Haunted House   150
The Haunted Duplex   151
The Ghost Train   153
The Lost Room   154
The Ghost of Deane House   155
Capitol Hill House   156
Canmore Opera House Ghost   157
Ghosts of Banff and Lake Louise   158

West Coast
The Ghost Photograph   165
The Headless Brakeman   166
The Chilliwack Poltergeist   167
The Spirit of the Hanging Judge   169
Pursuit by Lightning   170
The Oak Bay Hauntings   171
The Case of the Snoring Ghost   174
See the Dancing Indians   177
A Lady in the House   179
The Chinese Ghost   183
The "Twilight Zone" Truck Stop   185

The North
Mackenzie River Ghost   191
Spirit Rapping in the Far North   195
The Frozen City of the Yukon   196

Ghost Ship of the Arctic Sea   199
The Village of the Dead   200

Sources   207
Postface   221

Preface

Ghost Stories of Canada consists of one hundred accounts of encounters with ghosts that will thrill you and chill you!

Here are told-as-true stories of ghosts and spirits, poltergeists and hauntings, that are set in locales in all ten provinces and three territories of Canada. A handful of the stories are historical; the rest are contemporary. It is hoped that all the stories will make you "pause to wonder" about this world and the next.

I have tried to represent the major mysteries of the past. No collection of Canadian ghost stories would be complete without accounts of the Mackenzie River Ghost, the Baldoon Mystery, the Wynyard Apparition, the Great Amherst Mystery, or the Dagg Poltergeist. It is sad to say that these historical mysteries from the nineteenth century are better known outside the country than within Canada. Accounts have appeared and continue to appear in British and American publications; they are only now being discovered by Canadians. The past sheds light on the present. Alongside the tales of major mysteries are lesser-known mysteries from the last century and from the twentieth century — ghosts and hauntings of the here and now.

The real-life stories appear in six sections arranged from East to West to North: Maritimes, Quebec, Ontario, Prairies, West Coast, and The North. Within sections the stories appear in chronological order. I have tried to represent the regions of the country with respect to their relative populations. But foremost in my mind has been the desire "to tell a good story." I have tended to favour accounts that have appeared in print over the years, especially first-person accounts that make engrossing reading today.

Whether historical or contemporary, these accounts may be divided into two types: stories of the supernatural and stories of the paranormal. When I describe stories as "supernatural" I have in mind traditional narratives of local hauntings for which there were few if any named witnesses. Supernatural accounts have a glow about them — a wondrous, even miraculous, aura that renders them immune to the explanations of reason or science.

When I describe stories as "paranormal" I have in mind accounts that are told by named witnesses that presumably have some rational or scientific explanation but that the causation, currently beyond the known, will some day be explained by reason and science.

Perhaps one-third of the accounts are of the supernatural variety. They tell about fairies and phantom ships encountered in the Maritimes. They are inclined to be impersonal or "as told by." Perhaps two-thirds of the accounts are of the paranormal variety. In the main these are modern experiences and personal ones.

Are these stories true? Did these events happen? Are these experiences faithfully recalled? There is no way to answer in the affirmative; there is no reason to answer in the negative. No one was wittier than the rationalist George Bernard Shaw. He had occasion to review a book of ghost stories. In the course of the review he used the words "a classic ghost story"; what he then wrote was "a classic — therefore untrue — ghost story." Shaw stressed the noun *story* and not the adjective *ghost*. There is ambivalence to the word *story*; it refers to a narrative that may be imaginative or fictitious, real or true, or even "told as true." What Shaw had in mind is that some stories improve with the retelling. It is difficult to stick to the facts. And what are the facts?

The most interesting feature of the real-life ghost story is its physical implausibility coupled with its psychological plausibility. The story has a logic of its own. The story sets one thinking. It offers a sense of completeness, a sense of rightness. Dr. Samuel Johnson the lexicographer was attracted to them. All reason is against them, he noted, but all the emotions favour them.

Over the last twelve years I have edited one dozen books devoted to Canadian mysteries of the past and present. That is one book a year and about six hundred published accounts of ghosts and hauntings. So it is only reasonable that reviewers and interviews should ask me the question, "Do you believe in ghosts?"

I have a short answer to that question, and it seems to satisfy most readers. It goes like this: "Ghosts belong to the category of experience, not to the category of belief."

If I am pressed further, I explain that I have never seen a ghost or spirit, at least as yet, but that I seek out people who tell me that they have had these experiences. I am never sure whether they are lucky or unlucky. I make up my mind whether they are critical or credulous. I have little occasion to doubt their candour so I have no doubt that they believe they have seen or felt or sensed something that is unexpected and inexplicable, something that is often described as a ghost or a spirit. What I have noticed is that people who have had ghostly encounters hardly know what to make of these episodes. With high emotion they describe their experiences. Their accounts quite often begin, "You won't believe me when I say this but..." and they quite often end, "That's what happened to me. I do not know what to make of it...." In other words, most witnesses – most people who encounter ghosts – are quite ambivalent about the nature of the experience and the status of the spirits.

Practically everyone knows someone who admits to a peculiar and inexplicable experience. It may be a brother, sister, father, mother, aunt, uncle, neighbour, or acquaintance. More likely than not the witness will be more than willing to relate the experience, given suitable surroundings and sympathetic listeners. This is to be expected. People love to share their experiences, and an encounter with the unknown is a privileged adventure. In most older buildings there are creeking stairways that lead to musty attics. In old houses there are rooms with "cold spots" or "damp areas." There are summer cottages with doors on rusty hinges that will not fasten shut, and windows with billowy curtains that flutter in the absence of a breeze. There are bedrooms and basements and attics that have a special feeling about them. But I must admit no ghost has yet appeared to me. On occasion I have felt presences that other observers might describe as ghostly, and from time to time I have witnessed happenings that other people might consider having mysterious causes. So I am fascinated and satisfied with the experiences of others.

Ghosts may or may not exist, but one thing is certain: there is no shortage of ghost stories in Canada and elsewhere. The columns of nineteenth-century newspapers are a good source for accounts of hauntings that have hardly been tapped, and in this century tabloids and community papers offer the collector wonderful tales, especially around October 31, Halloween.

Books that collect real-life ghost stories are a modern invention. Traditional accounts of hauntings appear throughout history and cluster around famous people of the past. For instance, there are persistent accounts that Napoleon Bonaparte had a familiar spirit, whom he called his Red Man, who made unexpected appearances and advised and admonished him when least expected. Hauntings were the staple of newspapers and magazines, but it was not until the collections of Elliott

O'Donnell began to appear that the English-speaking world began to think in terms of collections of ghost stories. O'Donnell set the vogue for books with evocations of ghostly places. The Anglo-Irish writer visited Britain's haunted castles and country homes where he collected their haunting traditions and published them in a series of books from *Some Haunted Houses* (1908) to *Trees of Ghostly Dread* (1958). Peter Underwood of the Ghost Club has continued to publish books in the same vein. The latest development in the field is the appearance of books of "personal accounts" of the strange experiences reported by people who do not necessarily live in traditionally haunted places. I include in this category interviews with witnesses who have been favoured with sightings of flying saucers or unidentified flying objects. This development leads one to consider the possibility that it is people, rather than places, that are haunted.

One of the best of the English collections was *Lord Halifax's Ghost Book*, which appeared in 1936 and remains in print to this day. It includes the Mackenzie River Ghost; for many years that was the only account of a Canadian ghost known abroad. There did not seem to be any book about the mysterious in Canada until the appearance of *Exploring the Supernatural* in 1955. It was well-researched and movingly written by R.S. Lambert, as well it should, for its author was the founding editor of the BBC's influential magazine *The Listener* and a noted psychical researcher. He emigrated to Canada in 1939 and joined the CBC in Toronto for which, in later years, he served as director of School Broadcasts. He used all his abilities and talents to explain, in the words of the book's subtitle, "The Weird in Canadian Folklore."

Exploring the Supernatural was the first book in the field. *Psychic Mysteries of Canada* was the second. R.S. Lambert, the author of the first book, was a psychical researcher; A.R.G. Owen, the author of the second, is a mathematician and a geneticist as well as a parapsychologist. *Psychic Mysteries of Canada* appeared in 1975 and it is a thoroughgoing study of anomalous phenomena from the vantage point of sociology and psychology as well as parapsychology. Iris M. Owen, his wife, published *Conjuring Up Philip* the following year. It is truly "An Adventure in Psychokinesis" (the book's subtitle) for it examined the nature of the seance and established the interactive characteristics of hauntings. In essence, Lambert savoured the supernatural episodes; the Owens considered the parapsychological incidents.

The field widened in 1988 when I published *Mysterious Canada*, which described and documented five hundred of the country's major "mysteries," whether supernatural or parapsychological in nature, illustrated them, and offered balanced accounts for the general reader. Once it appeared I assessed the field of anomalous phenomena and realized that the strongest evidence for the existence of ghosts and UFOs, etc., lay in the personal experiences of men and women of all walks of life. These experiences take the form of narrative accounts, oral and written. I had collected a good many of these, but curious about how many of them there were "out there," I asked the editors of newspapers and community papers to run my letter to the editor inviting readers to write and send me accounts of their experiences. When I appeared on radio and television programs, I arranged for the interviewer to forward any communications from listeners and viewers. In this manner I accumulated vast files of first-person accounts. I call these accounts "memorates." Also, with the help of fellow researchers, I have collected "stories," that is, third-person accounts of mysteries that have appeared in the columns of newspapers in the past.

For a while I was all alone in this undertaking. Other collectors have begun to mine the traditions and publish collections of ghost stories. The main books that offer traditional and personal memorates and stories are listed in the bibliography.

I see mysteries and books of them as shedding light on human nature (and possibly inhuman nature) but also as interesting and intriguing components of Canadiana. (Mainstream Canadiana is marginal in North American life; imagine how marginalized is mysterious Canadiana!) Yet we have ghosts and spirits of our own, if only we would recognize them. There is no need for us to import them from foreign countries; "branch-plant" ghosts need not apply! Indeed, through my researches, I discovered that some of the world's most enduring mysteries have a strong if unrecognized Canadian component or connection. I have in mind such world mysteries as the curious abandonment on the high seas of the *Mary Celeste*, the birth of modern Spiritualism at the hands of the Fox Sisters, the haunting of Borley Rectory in England, and more.

Rather than reject ghosts or fear the unknown, we should embrace them. For this reason I adopted as my motto the following words: "Mysteries are good for us." There is no proof of the existence of ghosts and spirits, but there is plenty of evidence for their presence. The evidence takes the form of ghost stories. On the basis of such evidence, it is safe to conclude: Ghosts are good for us because they encourage us to face the greatest mysteries of all: life, death, fate, destiny, spirit, grace, damnation, salvation, deliverance, duty, and ... above all ... simple curiosity.

Acknowledgements

I have been helped along the way by a whole host of lively and kindred spirits.

Among the lively spirits who assisted me are friends, fellow investigators and researchers, editors, authors, and journalists who have written on the supernatural and the paranormal.

I am principally indebted to my friend Tony Hawke and his wife Liedewy who suggested that I add to my publications on mysteries a book of Canadian ghost stories.

M. Alice Neal, my researcher, has assisted me with this project as with previous undertakings over the last ten years. We made excellent use of the resources of the Toronto Reference Library, the Canadiana Department of the North York Central Library, and the CBC Reference Library. Dwight Whalen and W. Ritchie Benedict have continued to share with me their insights into Fortean phenomena, not to mention their clipping files.

Every collector of supernatural and paranormal Canadiana travels through forests and bush country, across tundra and taiga, over prairies and plains, upon rivers and lakes, following routes blazed by earlier collectors. I have in mind folklorists Helen Creighton and Edith Fowke; psychical researcher R.S. Lambert; parapsychologists George and Iris Owen; fellow editor Alberto Manguel; librarian Philip Singer; long-time friend Cyril Greenland; and others too numerous to mention.

Jillian Hulme Gilliland, the well-known artist and illustrator who lives in Kingston, Ont., kindly agreed to provide some lovely and charming drawings "to set the scene."

In the last decade a number of lively books have been published that gather together accounts of the country's ghosts. There are entries for the principal publications in "Sources."

Ruth Colombo, my own familiar spirit, has taken a position by my side to keep at bay the ghoulies and beasties!

MARITIMES

The Fairy Companion

The hoards of Fairy Folk hold hands with the host of Angelic Beings and find favour in the eyes of sensitive men and women, kindred spirits of the New Age in the New World.

It is a tradition hoary with age that fairies or Little People populate the country gardens and fields of heather of the British Isles. They are most likely to be seen in England, Scotland, Ireland, Wales, and Brittany; yet they are observed on rare occasions to prance in their peculiar way in circular fashion in the woods of the provinces of eastern Canada. Some fairy families are said to be populous and quite at home in the remoter regions of the Atlantic provinces — Newfoundland, Nova Scotia, New Brunswick, and Prince Edward Island. But they are not indigenous to this region. The earliest Scots settlers introduced them to these shores. Anyway, such is the tradition.

Here is a brief but fine passage about the fairy folk of Nova Scotia. It comes from W.Y. Evans-Wentz's impressive book *The Fairy-Faith in Celtic Countries.* An old man is speaking about his past:

My grandmother Catherine MacInnis used to tell about a man named Laughlin, whom she knew, being in love with a fairy-woman. The fairy-woman made it a point to see Laughlin every night, and he being worn out with her began to fear her. Things got so bad at last that he decided to go to America to escape the fairy-woman. As soon as the plan was fixed and he was about to emigrate, women who were milking at sunset out in the meadows heard very audibly the fairy-woman singing this song:

What will the brown-haired woman do
When Lachie is on the billows?

Lachie emigrated to Cape Breton, landing at Pictou, Nova Scotia; and in his first letter home to his friends he stated that the same fairy-woman was haunting him there in America.

About this traditional tale, first recorded among the Celtic traditions of Brittany in 1909, Evans-Wentz wrote, "To discover a tale so rare and curious as this ... is certainly of all our evidence highly interesting. And aside from its high literary value, it proves conclusively that the fairy-women who entice mortals to their love in modern times are much the same, if not the same, as the succubi of middle-age mystics."

How right was Evans-Wentz!

A Night with the Fairies

The fairy folk set foot on the rocky soil of Newfoundland and used it as a stepping-stone to the green landscapes of Nova Scotia, New Brunswick, and Prince Edward Island. They especially love the hills and dales of Cape Breton Island. We may not think that the little folk populate the New World, but they are there. All we need are eyes to see and ears to hear.

Here is a narrative recorded by folklorist Barbara Rieti in her book *Strange Terrain*. The speaker is a man from Colinet, a small community at the head of St. Mary's Bay. No doubt the experience is fictitious. Or is it?

It was March 1940. It was raining hard that night. Now I had no oil clothes or nothing, but still I was as dry as I am right now sitting here at this table. I left Mt. Carmel four o'clock in the evening and never reached home until one o'clock in the morning. I came to Colinet and travelled across the ice to John's Pond. I was on my way home from John's Pond to North Harbour and it was at the Beaver Pond that the fairies attacked me and took control of the horse. Whatever way I'd turn her, she'd head back toward John's Pond. The fairies would not let the horse leave the pond. So I tied the horse to a stump of a tree on the side of the pond. And you should hear the gibberish and singing all around me. It nearly sent me batty. No man would believe the singing, dancing, and music of these fairy characters. They were so handy they were within reach. When the cloud left, I put my head close to the water, and I saw little things on the side of the bank, around eighteen inches high, like rabbits. I tried to catch them, but they played all around me. They were teasing me. So I said, "Have your way, ye damn things." I left them alone and went back and lay on the sled. I was going to stay there the night. I stayed for so long and couldn't stand it any more. No prayer was any good. So I made oaths and swore on them. It was just like an orphanage when I started swearing. Such crying and screeching you could hear as the little creatures left and went eastward. The horse's eyes lit up the pond. When I finally got home, I untackled the mare from the sled and instead of going to the barn she headed right back up the hill again. I was from four o'clock to six o'clock in the rain, but still me cravat didn't have a speck of rain. After that the horse couldn't be held going across the pond. Others wouldn't ride her at all on the pond because she travelled so fast. Once she got off the pond, she was back to her own pace again.

The Phantom Trapper

Not everyone loves the landscape of Labrador. But many people do. The hills are granite, humbled by the glaciers of the distant past, and the only green to be seen comes from the stunted spruce trees that manage to survive in the land's many small dales. Four hundred years ago the harsh landscape was regarded with a cold eye and described with a chill pen by the French navigator Jacques Cartier as he sailed up the St. Lawrence River. In the account of his travels of 1534, he wrote the following melancholy words about the landscape: "In fine I am rather inclined to believe that this is the land God gave to Cain."

Indeed, the land is haunted by a Cain-like figure, an accursed wanderer, who from time to time is seen in the most deserted regions of this desolate land. He has no name but he is known as the Phantom Trapper. He is seen only in the winter. Those who have seen him describe him as a tall man, draped in animal skins. With great ferocity he drives his team of fourteen pure white huskies across the snow-covered tundra. He stops for no man.

Little is known of this spectre. The story is told that long ago there was a trapper who led a wicked and dissolute life. Despite his despicable acts, which included peddling poisoned alcohol to the Indians and assaulting local women, he was the despair of the constables and the object of the *curé's* prayers. The law was never able to catch up with him, and to his dying day he never repented of his crimes.

The Phantom Trapper died a natural death, but in death he found no rest. To atone for his sins, he was cursed by God to lead his dog team through the deep snows of winter throughout all eternity. The sight of the Phantom Trapper on his ghostly rounds is said to be a harrowing one. Yet Labradorians rejoice in the sight of this figure, for it seems he helps to guide lost travellers and trappers through blizzards to safety.

The Cain-like figure of the Phantom Trapper was last seen on his life-saving rounds in the year 1959.

The Fire-Ship of Northumberland Strait

Northumberland Strait is turbulent and it separates Nova Scotia and Prince Edward Island. Now spanned by the Confederation Bridge, it was once the domain of ferry-boats and the stage-setting for spectacular appearances of the Fire-Ship.

It is known as the Burning Ship or the Fire-Ship of Northumberland Strait. Here is an account of its sudden appearance told by Mrs. C.V., an informant from Halifax, Nova Scotia, who was living at the time of the sighting, about 1912, near Murray Harbour North, on the eastern end of Prince Edward Island.

＊·⇒◦◄◖⦿◗►◦⇐·＊

Now I will try to tell you just what I seen one afternoon the latter part of September. It was a beautiful day. There was not even a ripple on the water — no wind and the sun shining. I could see the shore of Cape Breton. I happened to look to my left and I seen a ship a long way away. It took about one-half hour as far as I could judge before I could see her good. When she came in full view I called my boy Fred (he was between seven and eight years) to come to me and see the vessel coming. Such a beautiful ship I never seen in my life. Something about her seemed different from other vessels. The sails seemed to be pure white and the ship seemed to be shining black. As it came nearer it seemed to lose speed, and as it came opposite our house it stopped still. I said to Fred, "Perhaps they are coming ashore." We got up on the banks to watch. There was no sign of anyone on board and no dory on tow. I can't remember just how long it was, but I think about ten minutes after she stopped I seen smoke rising very slow all over the deck. Then it was only a few minutes I seen men that seemed to come up from below and they were running around the deck every way. Then as they were running around I seen a low flame all over the deck. When the flames started the men climbed up the masts of the vessel. When they was about halfway up the masts the sails caught. All the sails seemed to catch at the same time. I could not see the men any more as the flames hid my view. We watched it until the flames died and everything crumbled to the deck. There was nothing left but the hull on the water, and gradually it seemed to sink lower and finally disappeared as if it gradually filled with water and sunk.

I had forgotten that I had heard of the burning ship. My brother happened to come to see us just as the spars crumbled. When I seen him coming I ran to meet him all excited for I thought it was a real ship. He said, "Carrie, have you forgotten about the ghost ship?"

The story is that that ship burned years ago and the belief is that it is the souls of those that perished by fire. The story is they were drinking below or asleep. It does not appear every year and not always at the same time. At that time there was no gasoline boats. When the gasoline boats came to that shore they tried to get near to it, but the most of them were too afraid to go too near as they said the heat from it was intense.... It seemed to me it was only half a mile off our shore.... My father used to take his powerful field glasses and watch it. He seen just what I seen.... Some fished there for years and never seen it.

The Phantom Ship of the Bay of Chaleur

The Phantom Ship of the Bay of Chaleur exists in story and song if not on the high seas. Catherine Jolicoeur began to collect ghost ship legends in 1960, and compiled over a thousand sightings from all over the world. She said: "People who see the Phantom Ship are not just imagining things. They certainly see something. One theory is that it's a kind of mirage; others think it's a marine phosphorescent manifestation."

She found a great many tales that tell about a phantom ship that haunts the Bay of Chaleur between Quebec and New Brunswick. One of the most interesting is this version, which adds a motif not common to reports of other phantom ships: that seeing it was a bad omen, foretelling a death. However, that belief was sometimes attached to the *Teazer*; Helen Creighton heard one person say: "If you see the *Teazer* you will die before the year is out."

This account was told by Mrs. Joseph Comeau of Carleton, Gaspé, Quebec.

In June 1912, when I was twelve years old, after three or four rainy days ... one foggy morning near a sandy shoal called Larocque Shoal I had the sudden impression of seeing an enormous ship coming between two rocky capes and moving. I cried, "Papa, look at the ship run aground there near the shore, scarcely three hundred feet from us."

My father said to me after a long silence, "That, my child, is the fire-ship, look at it well." It was indeed the shape of an enormous vessel with dark grey sails flecked with white. You could distinguish the masts, the sails, large and small. I saw no rudder or bow, it was all a big mass. I didn't see any people but instead some black shadows overlapped each other; they resembled bodies or barrels. I was thrown into confusion. It passed very quickly. After a good ten or fifteen minutes the famous ship advanced into the Bay of Chaleur with bigger waves, broke up, disintegrated, as though the hull, the sides, were eaten; finally it all disappeared from our sight, carried away by an enormous wave. My father seemed frightened by the apparition of the phantom ship.

We spoke of it at dinner. I recall that Papa spoke like this: "The first time that I saw it was the year that my father died; and another time, my brother died in the Klondike. This time I don't know what will happen within the year." In the month of October the same year, a little sister died....

July 1914, after a stormy night ... my brother and I saw a mass of black smoke, which seemed to have a long broad opening surface plunging into the most extensive of the two springs whose surface resembled a layer of water fifteen to thirty feet around. The rest of this mass was high, resembling a little mountain, taking different forms, swelling like sails. One would have said an animal whose sides moved in breathing. We were like jellyfish through fright, holding our breath. After quite a long time, at least half an hour, the black mass, as though satisfied, began to move, rocking, doubtless drawn by the sea, took the form of a great ship, releasing the sails, which we believed to be of smoke, and quietly launched itself into the sea between the two rocky capes.... Concerning this sight of the phantom ship we weren't allowed to tell these stories of the abnormal sights we'd seen; we had to keep the secret lest we be taken for superstitious people.

The Grey Lady of Annapolis Royal

Many years ago a small vessel sailed up the Annapolis Basin. On board was a lady dressed all in grey. Also on board was a deep-sea fisherman from this part of Nova Scotia who was employed to run ships to foreign ports. A few days later, when the small vessel returned and sailed down the Basin, the lady in grey was not to be seen. It was believed that the deep-sea fisherman, who was married with a family living in the region, brought this lady back with him from a foreign port. He knew not what to do with her, so he took her ashore at Stony Beach, on the Annapolis River, not far from the Habitation at Annapolis Royal, where he murdered her. He buried her body on the beach.

This is the Grey Lady who appears to walk on the beach from time to time. Men and women who have seen her say that on a few occasions she wears a short skirt, but that on most occasions she appears to be wearing a long gown, a shawl, and a bonnet. All are coloured grey. She glides along the shore. Her feet do not seem to touch the ground. Witnesses say she pauses from time to time, as if she wishes to unburden herself of the tragedy that has befallen her, but she disappears before a word can be spoken.

The Teazer Light

To see the Teazer Light, it is best to stand at Borgals Point on Mahone Bay, Nova Scotia. It is best to do so on a foggy night, within three days of a full moon, prior to a storm. If you are lucky, what you will witness is the sight of a burning ship a mile or two offshore. If you are standing on the deck of a ship at sea, the apparition of the fire-ship appears to threaten to ram your vessel. There are many reports of the Teazer Light, but there are no reports of instances of it causing any destruction, but when it appears, it strikes fear in the hearts of mariners.

Why is the effect known as the Teazer Light? On June 26, 1813, a privateer's vessel named *Young Teazer* was trapped by British warships in Mahone Bay. The British would have captured the vessel had it not been for one of the pirates who set his vessel on fire, preferring death on its deck to death on the yard-arm. Since then the Teazer Light has been observed on many foggy nights within three days of a full moon, prior to a storm, on Mahone Bay.

The Battle in the Sky

This story about a battle in the sky was recorded by the folklorist Sterling Ramsay. He identified the informant by his initials, G.S.P., and said that he was a Cape Bretoner. "This is a tale of an experience that befell a friend of mine, a truthful sailorman who is in no wise descended from the Ancient Mariner, and never has heard the Vision of Mirza. If anyone doubts the truth of the story, I can give you, as guarantee, the oath of the man with the dyed goatee who saw the schooner on which the sailorman had the experience." The tale of the battle in the sky is said to date from 1902.

On the 29th of July last we were anchored off Sydney Harbour, Cape Breton. Rain had fallen early in the morning but towards noon the weather changed to fine and the wind died away, so at our anchorage we had to stay for the rest of the day.

Shortly after 12:00 o'clock we had finished the dinner and to while away the time I went up on deck and stretched myself on the hatch preparatory to enjoying a good smoke.

I had hardly time to survey the view before me when I gazed upward, as though compelled, and almost immediately, in the sky above I beheld the most wonderful and beautiful phenomenon I have ever witnessed.

A cloud appeared to be scarcely a quarter of a mile away and in it were all the animals, birds, and reptiles that cover the earth. There were horses, cattle, sheep, pigs, lions, tigers, bears, wolves, dogs, cats, and numerous other animals I cannot name.

Some of the birds and reptiles proved very strange to me; more so as I have spent the greater part of my life on the sea and therefore am not much acquainted with the different species I saw. I thought at first the grand sight was all imagination, but to prove the contrary I called the crew to behold the sight.

All hands were soon on deck looking at the cloud, admiring in various ways its grandeur and beauty. No description can give any idea of the strangeness, splendour, and real sublimity of the sight. The Captain on beholding it said that it resembled the account given of the opening of the ark.

After a short time the cloud passed off to the east but was replaced by one that contained far greater marvel. This was a regiment of soldiers marching and singing the following as they marched:

Hurrah! Hurrah! for France!
Hurrah! Hurrah! for France!

We could hear it quite plainly as the cloud was moving about, and was nearer us than the other one had been. The Frenchmen gave way to another regiment of soldiers and these sang:

Hurrah! Hurrah! for England!
Hurrah! Hurrah! for England!
Hurrah! Hurrah! for England!

And Ireland, too!

As this regiment passed along another appeared and these sang:

Hurrah! Hurrah! for England!
Hurrah! Hurrah! for England!
Hurrah! Hurrah! for England!

And Bonnie Scotland, too!

As this regiment also passed along another appeared and these sang:

Hurrah! Hurrah! for England!
Hurrah! Hurrah! for England!
Hurrah! Hurrah! for England!

And the U.S., too!

Numerous other regiments passed along singing, also — as we could only understand English — we could not tell what country they represented.

The cloud now changed into a battlefield with its horses, guns, and soldiers, and the battle soon began. Each body of soldiers was dressed according to the custom of the country they hailed from. As we were all Scotchmen on board we took great interest in the Scotch regiments, the men of which were all dressed in kilts and were headed by a band of pipers.

The view was so magnificent and attractive that we never thought of taking notes at the time so we can only give a very meagre account of the battle.

We gazed at the grand spectacle till the sun had passed out of view in the golden west when the performance disappeared.

Next day we went ashore in Sydney and asked if any of the inhabitants had seen the sights that were visible in the clouds the day before. We were informed that no one had seen it.

The Ghost of Dr. Copeland's Wife

Sable Island is mainly sand dunes populated by wild horses. The island of shifting sands lies in the Atlantic Ocean about 300 kilometres southeast of Halifax, Nova Scotia. There are no permanent settlements, but the island has a long history of shipwrecked sailors, transported convicts, pirates on the run, and wreckers and salvagers. It has been called the "Graveyard of the Atlantic." It is described as an austerely grim place.

The slightly sinister island serves as the setting for the popular Maritime legend of the Ghost of Dr. Copeland's Wife. In 1802, it seems, the wife of a Dr. Copeland (both first names have been lost in the sweep of history) was sailing on the *Princess Amelia* when it ran against the rocks. Dr. Copeland drowned, but Mrs. Copeland was able to swim to shore. When the wreckers and salvagers arrived, they murdered her. Then they chopped off the third finger of her left hand to steal her wedding ring, which they could not otherwise remove.

Since then, at intervals of fifty years, the ghostly figure of Dr. Copeland's Wife appears. The figure is that of a middle-aged woman, dressed in white, and it is seen to drift up and down the shifting sands of the beach. The woman in white is presumably searching for her missing finger and its wedding ring, if not for revenge.

The *Fairie Queene*

A strange story is told of the fate of the passengers aboard the *Fairie Queene.*

Without cause or reason, the bell of St. James Church in Charlottetown, Prince Edward Island, tolled a total of eight times, early Friday morning, October 7, 1859.

After five tolls, two men who lived in the vicinity went to investigate. They were startled when the bell tolled for the sixth time and the church doors were suddenly flung open and inside stood three women dressed in white. Just as suddenly the bell tolled for the seventh time and the doors swung shut. They tried the doors only to find them locked. Peering through a small window, they could see a lone woman in white ascend the stairs to the belfry.

By this time the minister and sexton had arrived to learn the cause of the disturbance. They unlocked the doors and together the four men entered and found not a living soul in the body of the church. But as they made their way up the stairs to the belfry, they heard the bell toll for the eighth and last time. They found no one in the belfry and the bell-rope was securely tied. Everyone was puzzled.

That evening they were equally perplexed when the *Fairie Queene* failed to arrive at the Charlottetown wharf. The passenger steamer regularly plied the Northumberland Strait between Nova Scotia and Prince Edward Island. They learned that it had left Pictou and they knew that it was fine sailing weather. But the vessel never arrived at Charlottetown, a run of no more than half a day. It was some days before they learned that the vessel had sunk with the loss of eight passengers, five men and three women.

Had the bell of St. James Church foretold the disaster? Was its tolling a coincidence? Is it all a legend? "That mystery remains unsolved to this day," noted writer Roland H. Sherwood.

The *Charles Haskell*

This is the story of the "hoodoo ship" known as the *Charles Haskell*.

The *Charles Haskell* was a Boston fishing schooner. It seemed headed for trouble even before it was launched. When it was being outfitted for cod fishing off the Grand Banks, a workman slipped on the companionway and broke his neck. Now sailors are a suspicious lot, and they have long memories, so this was not an auspicious beginning for the fishing vessel. It was shunned by crews. Its maiden voyage was marred when the captain refused at the last minute to take it out, and a substitute captain had to be hastily found.

But fate had an interesting role for the *Charles Haskell* to play. Fate would turn it into one of the best known "hoodoo ships," a vessel that seems doomed from brave start to inglorious finish. The following tragic accident occurred on March 7, 1866, off Georges Bank, where the *Haskell* was at anchor. It seems that there was a sudden storm at sea. The captain of the *Haskell* was concerned that he and his crew would be engulfed in the storm. Then he observed the rapid approach of another fishing vessel, the *Andrew Jackson* of Salem, Massachusetts. He gave orders to cut anchor, with the result that the *Haskell*, cut loose, rammed the *Jackson*, which sank with all hands on board. The *Haskell* sustained some damage but there was no recorded loss of life. It limped back to St. John's harbour.

The following spring it was taken back to the Georges Bank and after six days out something inexplicable occurred. Two men on the midnight watch were alarmed when they observed the bobbing of human heads in the sea all around the *Haskell.* The heads became bodies as the men in oilskins, streaming with water, silently slipped over the rails. They took their places on the deck and spoke not a word. They had no eyes, merely empty sockets. The two horrified men called for the captain and he too observed the ghostly crew. In all, twenty-six phantom sailors took up positions along the rail and went through the motions of baiting and sinking. They engaged in this activity all night long, but with the approach of dawn, they silently slipped over the rails and returned to the depths of the sea.

The same thing happened the following night. At dusk the spectral sailors appeared and fished until dawn. But this time, when they slipped over the rails, they did not return to the sea. Instead, when they left the vessel, their boots rested on the brine and they walked across the waves in a grim, mute procession in the direction of Salem, Massachusetts.

The *Haskell* returned to St. John's, and word got around that it was a "hoodoo ship." No sailor would agree to set foot on its decks. Consequently, it was tied to the wharf and abandoned by its owners. Not long after it was towed out to sea and burnt to the waterline. Such was the fate of the *Charles Haskell,* in fame or in infamy, a "hoodoo ship."

Mr. Extry Man

Some ghosts are menacing figures, others are helpful figures. Here is the story of a spirit that returned from the dead to help the crew of a ship. The spirit turns up as an extra hand that is needed, even though his death was caused by the mate.

The story is told in nautical language by Horace Johnson of Port Wade, Nova Scotia. It is not necessary to know the meanings of all the sailor's terms to appreciate the salty tang of the tale. The word "hanted" is used here for "haunted."

About fifty years ago when my brother was captain of the *Vesta Pearl,* I sailed with him as mate. The captain takes care of the after end of the ship and the mate the forward end. Well, this vessel was built in St. John, and that's where we bought her, and after we got her they said she was a hanted vessel. One old fellow said, "You can't run her, she hanted." So I said, "If she's hanted now she's hanted so bad she's got to keep moving."

The crew didn't want to stay aboard after the word got around. Someone told them the last captain had been knocked overboard when she was new and on her first trip and that he'd been drowned, but none of us knew the whole story. All we knew was that he was always around. He'd be there in a gale of wind when we were reefing the sails. If four men were reefing and one was at the wheel, there would be one man at the wheel and five men reefing, but you had to be at the wheel to see him.

He didn't bother us until we'd been out four months. We got caught in an easterly wind going to Boston and we were bobbing in the sea and when we went to reef, there was Mr. Extry Man. My brother called me to come and take the wheel. He said, "I'd rather go and help reef," but he didn't tell me why. It was then I found out about the extry man. I saw him for myself.

One time when we were in Annapolis we got rigged up [dressed up] and went ashore. It didn't take much to dress you up in those days. On account of the tide the boat was high up in the water and we figured out the tide to see what time we should come back. Tides are mighty high here and when it was out we could walk right out to the boat but it would be muddy going. Then you could climb up the ladder and on to the ship's deck. If we stayed ashore too long we couldn't walk back to her.

I had my rubber boots waiting on the shore and when I got back I put them on and made my way to the ship. The tide was getting pretty well up to the vessel when I got there, and I figured that the other men wouldn't be able to get back without a boat till the next tide. I shook my feet to get the mud knocked off my boots, and scraped them on every rung of the ladder.

It seems that anybody going to sea, it makes no odds whether they've had their supper or not, because when they come aboard they always have to have a mugup, hot or cold. This night I was the only one aboard and I was having a mugup. Tea, it was. They had a lot of salt horse [salt beef] aboard this vessel and I was quite hungry because I'd gone without eating from six to eleven.

Well, I was having my mugup and salt horse when I heard another fellow coming stomping same as I did and, when he reached the deck, he seemed to go forward. So I says, "My gracious, he just made it," because the tide was pretty well around the vessel. I could tell because while I was setting there the ship riz and I could feel her come up out of the mud. I said to myself, "Who's that come aboard?" because after I heard him stomping I didn't see no more nor hear nothin', but I'd heard him all right because he scraped his boots off the same as I done. So I took the lantern to see where he walked because I knew the mud would show his tracks, but nothing showed.

Well, the watch had gone off when I come aboard and I knew I was alone and I don't know whether I was frightened or not, but it was a little bit of a strange kind of feeling. I thought somebody might have gone overboard but I couldn't see nothin' with the lantern and, when the others came back, I asked, and it hadn't been them. So it must-a been him — The Extry Man....

Later we were told the reason for it all. It seems that when the company was building this vessel they didn't know which of two fellows to give it to and, after they finally made up their minds, the fellow who lost went as mate. He was steering the wheel when the captain went over. He was probably working on the deck when the wheelsman gave it a sudden turn and sent the captain over the side. It was always thought he done it a-purpose.

Joshua Slocum's Ghost

Joshua Slocum was the Maritime sea captain who became the first person to sail alone around the world. He accomplished the first solo circumnavigation of the Seven Seas in 1895-98 aboard the *Spray*, a converted oyster boat only thirty-six feet in length.

Slocum was a crusty old soul. He was born in the village of Westport on Brier Island off the end of Digby Neck at the entrance to the Bay of Fundy. Thus, water surrounded him from the day of his birth to the day of his death, yet he never saw the need to learn to swim.

Joshua Slocum's ghost is not the ghost of the master mariner and seafarer, but the ghost he saw aboard the *Spray* on its three-year trip around the world. It was an altogether strange and uncharacteristic incident. In July 1895, Slocum ran into squally weather between the

Azores and Gibraltar. At the same time he was afflicted with severe stomach cramps and had to abandon the wheel and go below to rest.

He slept for some time below and upon returning to the deck he was astonished to see at the helm a tall, foreign-looking sailor! Where had he come from?

"Señor," the figure said, "I have come to do you no harm." It smiled and added, "I am one of Columbus' crew, the pilot of the *Pinta*, come to aid you. Lie quiet, señor captain, and I will guide your ship tonight."

Slocum did as he was advised and the next day, with the return of fair weather and better health, he found that the Spray was exactly on course, despite the fact that there was no one at the helm — except the foreign-looking phantom!

In the memoirs that he subsequently wrote, Slocum explained, "Columbus himself could not have held her more exactly on her course. I felt grateful to the old pilot ... I had been in the presence of a friend and a seaman of vast experience."

That was Slocum's sole experience with a ghost. Yet his death was the kind of death that only fate could determine. Slocum was sixty-six years old and in excellent health when he outfitted the *Spray* for another long, solo voyage. The outfitting was done at the yard at Bristol, Rhode Island. Asked where he was heading, he replied, "Some far away places." Sure enough, on November 14, 1909, he set sail from Martha's Vineyard. No one ever saw Slocum or the *Spray* again.

"Missing at sea" may not be a mysterious way to describe an accident or misadventure on the high seas, but the question should be asked, "Why did Slocum and the *Spray* disappear?" After all, it happened between Bristol and Grand Cayman in the Atlantic Ocean in the "region of mysteries" which the writer Charles Berlitz would later call "the Bermuda Triangle"!

The Codfish Man

If you are strolling around the harbour of West Saint John, New Brunswick, and if it is the evening of April 18, you may be lucky and behold the sight of the Codfish Man.

Watch out for an old man clad in oilskins and sou'wester, who is trudging up from the wharves carrying a giant codfish over his shoulder, a cod so huge it hangs down his back and forces him to walk slightly bent forward.

There is the belief that if you follow him, you can catch up with him. But just as you are about to do so, he disappears and then reappears some thirty feet ahead. Later that evening you may meet him again, sauntering back to the harbour, without the giant codfish.

If you want to know more about him, details are pretty sketchy. But the Codfish Man is believed to be the spectre of Daniel Keymore, a fisherman in the days of sail. An unexpected gale hit the Bay of Fundy on April 18, capsizing his boat. He drowned, to the sorrow of his wife and young children who lived in a small house in West Saint John. It seems that every year on the anniversary of his death, a giant cod was deposited on the doorstep of his house, to the astonishment of his widow. The gifts from the sea continued to arrive until she remarried some years later.

The Colonel's Ghost

The Prince's Lodge is a Halifax landmark that overlooks Bedford Basin. The lodge is a reconstruction of the original domed music room that was designed and erected in 1794 at the request of Prince Edward, Duke of Kent, the future father of Queen Victoria.

In July of the following year, the Prince and his consort Madame de St. Laurent hosted a brilliant reception for three hundred officers and their guests. The lodge was suitably decorated and never looked more splendid. But an event that occurred that evening earned it the reputation of being a ghostly haunt.

It seems that during the festivities, a certain Colonel and a certain naval Officer, having drunk more than their fill of brandy, exchanged words. They had to be restrained by their companions. In the custom of the day, the Colonel and the Officer agreed to meet a few hours hence, at two o'clock the next morning, at the cove south of the Round House. They arrived separately, armed with swords, and accompanied by fellow Officers who agreed to serve as seconds. Contrary to Army and Navy regulations, they entered into a duel. There was thrusting and parrying and there were flesh wounds. But one of the wounds proved to be more than a flesh wound. The Colonel faltered, reeled, and died. He was later buried without military honours.

To this day the Colonel's ghost is said to appear in the vicinity of the Prince's Lodge. If you wish to see him at two o'clock in the morning, the place to be is near the cove south of the Round House, where the fatal duel was fought. He is seen to falter, reel, and expire.

The Wynyard Apparition

Historical mysteries are a particular delight. They are a delight to me — and I hope to you — because when we read about them in the yellowed pages of old books or the tattered columns of old newspapers, we learn a lot about ghosts and apparitions, to be sure. But at the same time, we learn not a little about some facts of history, custom, tradition, and the beliefs of the past.

The Wynyard Apparition is an historical mystery that grew out of an incident that is said to have occurred in the year 1785 in Sydney, Cape Breton Island, Nova Scotia.

It involves an apparition, not a ghost. An apparition is the appearance of a living person at a distance. The living person is often someone who is at the point of death, or someone who is experiencing some other crisis, who wishes to communicate his or her plight to a loved one in another part of a house, a town, a country, a continent, or the world. So an apparition is a spectre-like "double." In this way it differs from a ghost, which is the spirit of a person already dead; the person may be known or unknown, it does not matter.

The Wynyard Apparition is one of the world's best-known "crisis apparitions." The story has been told many times, but that does not stop me from telling it one more time, based on the facts that were supplied by A. Patchett Martin in volume one of his book, *Life and Letters of the Right Honourable Robert Lowe, Viscount Sherbrooke* (1893).

Can the apparition of a man at death's door appear to walk through a door half a world away? Your answer to that question depends on what you think happened about four o'clock of the afternoon of October 15, 1785, in the quarters of Lieutenant George Wynyard of the British Army stationed in Sydney, Cape Breton Island, Nova Scotia.

The incident involves two people ... or three people, if you want to regard the spectre that appears as a person. They are the above-mentioned

George Wynyard, who was later appointed General, and Captain John C. Sherbrooke, later Lieutenant-Governor of Nova Scotia and, later still, Governor of Canada (1816-18). As for the spectre ... read on!

Wynyard and Sherbrooke, young officers, were seated in Wynyard's quarters, drinking wine and probably smoking, staring into the blazing fire in the fireplace, as good friends do. It is important to visualize the sitting-room in which they were sitting and to understand the positions of the room's two doors. One of the doors opened into an outer passageway; the other door opened into the bedroom. There were no windows.

Sherbrooke looked up to see a tall youth, about twenty years old, pale and worn, standing beside the closed door that led to the passageway. The figure was wearing some sort of newfangled hat. He was astonished. He had not seen or heard the door open and close. He thought he was alone in the room with Wynyard.

He called Wynyard's attention to the tall figure. Wynyard looked and turned deathly pale.

"I have heard of a man being pale as death," Sherbrooke later said, "but I never saw a living face assume the appearance of a corpse, except Wynyard's at that moment."

Neither one said a word. While they looked on, incredulously, the tall figure turned its gaze upon Wynyard and gave him a glance that mingled sorrow and affection. After doing this, it glided across the room, passing between the two friends and the fireplace and right through the bedroom door.

Wynyard seized his friend's arm and said in a hoarse whisper, "Great Heavens! My brother!"

"Your brother?" replied Sherbrooke. "What do you mean? There must be some deception; let us follow."

They instantly rose from the chairs, raced across the sitting-room, opened the door, and entered the bedroom. They found it empty. The windows of the bedroom had been puttied and bricked shut to keep out the cold.

How had the young man entered the sitting-room? How had he entered the bedroom? Where was he now?

They returned to the sitting-room and scratched their heads in disbelief. Wynyard must be mistaken. The tall figure could not be Wynyard's brother. If it was, how possibly could Wynyard's brother appear in the sitting-room, when all along he was living in England?

At that moment there was a knock on the door. It was Ralph Gore, an officer friend, who was told what had happened. He questioned his friends and then conducted his own search of the premises. When he found nothing, he urged his friends to prepare a memorandum about the strange event, and this is what Sherbrooke did.

In those days the mail was brought from England by packet-boat. There was no mail for Wynyard on the next packet, but there was one letter that was addressed to Sherbrooke. He hastily opened it and read it. He avoided Wynyard and sought out a mutual friend and in a low voice told him: "Wynyard's brother is dead!"

The first line of the letter went like this: "Dear John, Break to your friend Wynyard the death of his favourite brother."

It transpired that John Otway Wynyard had died in England. Moreover, he had expired at the very moment that his apparition had appeared at his brother's door.

The mail-boat brought some badly needed clothes. Included was a man's hat of the latest design. The newfangled hat was the spitting image of the one worn by the tall youth.

So it seems the apparition of a man at death's door can appear to walk through a door half a world away.

The Great Amherst Mystery

A Canadian Tire store stands at the corner of Princess and Church streets in downtown Amherst, Nova Scotia. There should be a plaque there to mark the location of the Cox family cottage, which stood at 6 Princess Street. After all, in 1878-79, it was the site of the Great Amherst Mystery, one of the world's most widely reported hauntings.

I am not going to retell the fascinating story here because it would take too long. Besides, I have told it elsewhere. It took me some four thousand words to summarize it in *Mysterious Canada*. Suffice it to say that a poltergeist was busy at the two-storey, wooden cottage that was inhabited by eight members of the family including eighteen-year-old Esther Cox, who was in poor health and unhappy in love. Esther had troubled dreams, and her limbs would seem to swell to enormous size. Bedclothes would fly through the air. One night these words appeared on the bedroom wall in large characters: "Esther Cox, you are mine to kill." Then there were pounding sounds and loud retorts heard throughout the house. Witnesses from the community heard these noises and attested to the fact that the house rocked on its foundation. Then small fires broke out in uninhabited rooms. Whenever Esther left the house the disturbances ceased. She finally left for good and later married, had children, and found peace. There is no doubt that she was the focus of the poltergeist disturbances but no one ever confronted her actually causing the manifestations.

So much for the Great Amherst Mystery. Intriguingly, many of the disturbances at the Cox family cottage in the 1870s were precisely recreated at Borley Rectory, Essex, England, in the 1930s. There is evidence to show that the haunted house in Amherst set the pattern for the events reported at Borley, "the most haunted house in England." Rather than trace the threads in that pattern, I would prefer to share with readers an almost entirely unknown description of Esther Cox. It comes from an interview with the young woman that appeared in the *Daily Sun* (Saint John, N.B.), June 23, 1879.

Miss Esther Cox, the spirit medium, commonly known as the "Amherst mystery," arrived here in care of friends on Friday afternoon last, and a detailed account of the manifestations and workings of "the mystery" were given in Ruddock's Hall on Friday evening and Saturday. Sunday evening, Miss Cox essayed to attend service at the Baptist Church, but during the first singing "the spirit," which had been quiet for some days, again manifested itself by rapping, apparently on the floor of the pew in front. When told to stop by Miss Cox it would cease the noise for a moment, but then break out worse than ever. Throughout the prayer it continued, and when the organ began for the second singing the noise became so distinct and disturbing that Miss Cox and party were forced to leave the church. Upon reaching the house on Wesley Street, where they were stopping, "the spirit" seemed to enter into Miss Cox, and she was sick and insensible until morning. Lying upon the bed she seemed for a time as though in great pain, her chest heaving as though in a rapid succession of hiccoughs — and the body and limbs being very much swollen. A medical gentleman of this town, who saw her at this time, states that the symptoms were as those of a functional heart disease, probably caused by nervous excitement.

41

The heart was beating at an exceedingly rapid rate and the lungs seemed gorged with blood, so that a portion was forced into the stomach, causing the patient to vomit blood afterwards. A sound could be distinctly heard in the region of the heart, resembling the shaking of water in a muffled bottle, supposed to be caused by blood in a cavity being shaken by the violent jerking, hiccoughy motion of the body. As to the cause of the affliction, that is the mystery.

Towards morning Miss Cox relapsed into a state of somnolence, and later in the day woke seemingly entirely recovered. She states, however, that on Monday afternoon, while sitting near the window of a room on the ground floor, a fan dropped out of the window. She went outside to recover it, and on returning, a chair from the opposite side of the room was found upside down near the door, as though it had attempted to follow her out of the room. No one else witnessed this occurrence. Again, while writing a letter, "the spirit" took possession of the pen and wrote in a different hand altogether, other and entirely different words from what were intended. In fact it wrote of itself, the young lady being able to look in another direction and not show the least interest in what the pen was writing. A gentleman who was present at the time asked "the spirit" its name, when it wrote in reply "Maggie Fisher," and stated that she had gone to "the red school-house on the hill in Upper Stewiacke" before Miss Cox did, but left when she went. Miss Cox did not know this Maggie Fisher, but it seems that one time she did attend the school indicated, and that a girl of that name, now dead, had attended previously.

Monday night Miss Cox was again attacked, and held under the power of "the spirit" much the same as the night previous.

A representative of the "Despatch" called on "the mystery" yesterday afternoon, but she not being "under the power" of course no "manifestations" could be seen. The young lady appeared quite pleasant and affable, and looked well. She considers her trouble to be a spirit, and is more perplexed with it than any one else. She says that she cannot tell by any premonitory symptoms when the manifestations are going to commence, is becoming rather frightened concerning "it," and is very easily annoyed and excited by any noise except that which she herself may cause.

If the spirit is willing and the flesh not too weak, Miss Cox will leave for Chatham by train today.

The Fire-Spook of Caledonia Mills

Students of Canadian mysteries are familiar with what has been called the Fire-Spook of Caledonia Mills. Between 1899 and 1922, the MacDonald Homestead at Caledonia Mills, a small community of the Highland Scots located south of Antigonish, Nova Scotia, was subjected to terrific, poltergeist-like effects. There were strange lights, peculiar noises, mysterious fires, unexplained movements of animals and household articles, etc.

During the winter of 1922 these effects were studied by the well-known Maritime detective P.O. (Peachy) Carroll, from Pictou, and Dr. Walter Franklin Prince, principal research officer of the American Society for Psychical Research. Prince's expenses from New York were borne by the Halifax *Herald* in exchange for exclusive coverage of the investigation. Carroll and Prince, working independently, came to the conclusion that the cause of the manifestations was Mary Ellen MacDonald, the adopted daughter, who had no knowledge that she was the agency through which the effects were made manifest. In the parlance of psychical research, she was the "focus" of the poltergeist effects.

Here is an account of a visit to the site of the famous mystery written by N. Carroll Macintyre, a native of Antigonish.

Growing up in the Town of Antigonish, most people were always interested in the stories about the Spook Farm. It was in the fall of 1961 that I had my first opportunity to visit the MacDonald homestead. A friend of mine, Art Farrell from Glencoe (across the woods from Caledonia), promised me a trip to the historic site. In preparation for the occasion, I asked questions and read any material that was available in order that I might fortify myself for the adventure.

On a sunny Saturday afternoon, I was formally escorted to the Spook Farm by Art Farrell, Ed MacDonald from Salmon River, and our driver from Roman Valley who was also to be our tour guide. Since Roman Valley is the next community to Caledonia Mills, we were assured that our guide was well familiar with the area. We boarded his old Jeep and made the trip through the woods to the homesite. As we drew near the location we were warned just to look about and not touch anything or take any souvenirs. He told us several stories about the farm, some of which I knew to be true, while others had the distinct flavour of local folklore. Being a "townie," I was subjected to more jibs and jabs than the others.

Upon arriving at the location of the farm, I was immediately disappointed. There was no haunted house, no barns — they had all fallen down years ago. There were just indentations in the ground where they once stood. As I wandered about the area, I tried to reconstruct the strange occurrences of the winter of 1922. I did not experience anything "eerie" (which I was well prepared for); it just appeared to be another old deserted plot of land that could be found in any rural area of Antigonish Country.

We were told by our guide, "Don't touch nothing." Having ventured to the area of mystery, it was my decision not to leave the old homestead without a souvenir, no matter how minuscule it might be. When no one was looking, I stuffed a piece of burnt shingle, which I had dug up from around the foundation, into my back pocket. We finally completed our investigation of the area and boarded the Jeep for the trip back to the main road.

As we approached the half-way point in our journey to the main road, our guide stopped the Jeep and asked if anyone had taken anything from the farm. Not wanting to give up my souvenir and hoping that it was just a whim on his part, I immediately answered no. We then proceeded. As we drew nearer to the main road, the Jeep was once again stopped, and the same question was asked. Our guide was not satisfied with the answer of no, and refused to move. Without warning, he turned towards me and said, "Macintyre, you took something." Of course I remembered the shingle in my back pocket, and produced it. The Jeep was turned around, and we returned to the farm, where I was asked to replace it, which I did.

Many would pass this off as normal, but to me it was a touch of the abnormal. I was pleased with the experience; at least I had something to tell about when I returned home. It was several years later, when I mentioned the occurrence to the noted folklorist C.I.N. MacLeod, that he stated some people had the "Celtic feeling," and when certain people visited such a location, they were able to draw out of the area a type of extrasensory perception. It appeared that our man from Roman Valley had that feeling and caused the return of my souvenir.

Evidently I did not learn my lesson....

It was probably the poltergeistic aspect of the Fire-Spook of Caledonia Mills, always in the back of my mind, that prompted me to chronicle the events that took place on the MacDonald homestead from 1899 to 1922. That aspect had to do with my last visit to the farm, the first week of May 1971.

I was asked by one of the senior members of the Casket Printing and Publishing Company Ltd., Eileen Henry, to give her a tour of the Spook Farm. As it was ten years since I had visited the site, I was only too glad to oblige. Of course I wanted to see for myself the changes that had taken place in the area during the past decade.

On a sunny, Saturday afternoon, we parked the car at the end of the lane heading up to the farm. It was considerably more difficult to find the actual site as it had grown over. However, after some misses, we arrived at the precise location where the house once stood. I gave Mrs. Henry an impromptu tour of the area and reconstructed some of the events that had taken place some fifty years previous. Of course, I added a few stories that were well-laced with local folklore. I remember Eileen distinctly hanging on to my arm all the way back to the car.

I could not resist the temptation to dig about a bit in the area of the old foundation. To my surprise I came across an old-fashioned, hand-painted egg cup that had resisted the test of years underneath a board.

I should have learned from my experience years earlier — the shingle episode — and left well enough alone, but for me the temptation was too great. I placed the egg cup carefully in my pocket, and took it away from the homesite of Alexander "Black John" MacDonald. That evening, after returning to Antigonish, I drove down to our summer farmhouse at Frog Hollow. When I arrived I realized that I still had the egg cup in my pocket. I decided that a small shelf in the kitchen would be the proper resting place for my new-found treasure. I knew that it would be a good conversation piece, and on many occasions late at night would lend itself to a good ghost story. However, this was not to be.

On the Victoria Day weekend, a few Saturdays later, I held the first gathering of the summer season at the farmhouse. The Saturday night affair was enlivened by the addition of the egg cup. The result was that numerous stories were told of Mary Ellen the Spook. Of course, as the evening wore on (as well as the refreshments), the stories got better and spookier. It seemed that the egg cup was the centre of attraction that evening.

Around 1:30 a.m., my guests began to leave, and by 2:00 a.m. there remained myself and two friends to help clean up. It would have been about 2:45 a.m. when we finished — dishes were done, ashtrays emptied, fires put out, et al. A suggestion was made by Dubie that rather than go back to town we stay the night at the house, as it was quite late (early) and we were all well "under the weather." I remember that I was quite adamant about the fact that the beds would be damp and we would "catch our death" if we stayed the night. As I had the only transportation back to town, my friends had to concede and return to town with me. Was it some premonition on my part that we did not stay in the house that night, or was it that I was just plain scared that we would "catch our death"?

Three and a half hours later, at 6:15 a.m., I returned to Frog Hollow, as Antigonish Harbour was popularly known. The only thing left standing of the once-lovely old farmhouse was the chimney. It had burnt to the ground! Would we have "caught our death" if we had stayed the night?

The Little Man Who Wasn't There

There is no shortage of haunted houses in the Maritimes, or of ghosts and spirits who are there one night and gone the next!

The town of Antigonish had its own haunted house in 1898, and psychical researchers came to investigate from Boston and New York. Stories of the elusive ghost made the newspapers in the Maritime provinces and the New England states. The stories reached New York and inspired a versifier named Hughes Mearns to pen a four-line verse, a ditty really, which has remained in memory to this day, long after the ghost that inspired it has vanished for good and even the haunted house has long been torn down.

The title of Mearns's verse is "Antigonish." It goes like this:

As I was going up the stair
    I met a man who wasn't there!
He wasn't there again today!
    I wish, I *wish* he'd stay away!

Hughes Mearns (1875-1965) was an American educator and versifier. The figure of an elusive "man who wasn't there" appealed to Mearns and inspired him. He wrote the verse on March 27, 1922, but there is some question about whether or not it refers to a haunting in 1898 or to one in 1922. Little matter.

What is of interest, however, is the fact that Mearns went on to pen a sequence of parodies with the general title "Later Antigonishes." Here is the best of them, a parody called "Alibi": As I was falling down the stair / I met a bump that wasn't there; / It might have put me on the shelf / Except I wasn't there myself."

"Antigonish" has given delight to generations of readers who enjoy the ghostly paradox of wishing away someone who is really not there. Curiously, it is Mearns's verse that refuses to go away!

The Phantom Train of Bras d'Or

They still speak of the Phantom Train of Bras d'Or. Its tracks ran beside St. Andrews Channel, Cape Breton Island, Nova Scotia. Mary L. Fraser, a Roman Catholic sister and folklorist, tells its story in the words of a number of informants.

————

Some years ago, people who live on a certain hill at Barrachois, Cape Breton, used to watch a phantom train glide noiselessly around the headlands of the Bras d'Or, and come to a stop at a gate leading to one of the houses. One who saw it herself told me how at seven o'clock every evening for a whole month every family on the hill would go out of doors to see it. Every coach was lighted, but no people could be seen. At the hour of its approach, some people sometimes went down to the track to get a better look at it, but were disappointed at its not coming at all, although the watchers on the hill saw it as usual. At the end of the month, a man was killed by a train just at the gate to which the phantom train used to come. Nobody saw it afterwards.

Haliburton House

There is an old saying that it is hard to keep a good man down. Judge Haliburton was just such a good man. Irrepressible in life, he may also be inexhaustible in death.

Thomas Chandler Haliburton was born in Windsor, Nova Scotia, and became a prominent magistrate and prosperous author. In 1834-35, he erected an attractive wooden villa, now known as Haliburton House, on an estate of twenty-five acres. Here, at the age of forty, he penned his influential satire *The Clockmaker* (1836). He died at Isleworth, England, in 1865.

Haliburton House now serves as a provincial museum, but the villa and its grounds have a long history of being haunted. Perhaps the earliest ghost is that of a kilted piper, a member of the Black Watch. It seems the regiment was marching across the property when its piper accidentally dropped his timepiece into the pond. Leaning over to retrieve it, he lost his balance, fell in, and drowned. At least he was never seen again. But to this day the body of water is known as Piper's Pond. Folklorist Helen Creighton reports that local children were told that if they ran around the pond twenty times, a soldier would emerge from its depths on horseback. The children ran nineteen times around but lost their courage on the twentieth. Since those years the pond has been drained.

Former residents of Haliburton House claimed that it was haunted by Judge Haliburton. On a number of occasions his ghost was seen to emerge from a secret panel in the wall of the reception hall. The spirit would wander around the hall for some time before passing back through the panel.

Hopper's Headstone

Restless spirits, yes. But what about restless headstones?

There is a tradition of a restless headstone in an old cemetery on Deer Island, New Brunswick. Deer Island lies north of Campobello Island between Passamaquoddy Bay and the Bay of Fundy.

The headstone is that of John Hopper, a strong-willed farmer who suffered bouts of depression. After two suicide attempts, he succeeded in drowning himself in a pond in the pasture beyond his farmhouse. In life he had made it known that in death he wished there to be no grave marker. Despite his express wishes, neighbours who buried the body at an appropriate site near the pond raised a headstone over his burial place. The simple inscription read as follows: "John Hopper / 5 May 1850."

Apparently Hopper's headstone will not stand of its own accord. It always topples down. If someone sets it right, in three days' time it will be found to be knocked over again. Once a neighbour cemented it in place, but three days later it was found to be cracked in two.

Hopper's spirit is restless. And so is his headstone!

The Dungarvon Whooper

The story of the Dungarvon Whooper has been called "the storied Miramichi country's greatest ghost story."

The Dungarvon River runs through central New Brunswick, a well-storied region. One Sunday in winter in the late 1860s, at a logging camp along the river, an Irish-born logger known as Young Ryan invited the camp's cook to accompany him on a hunting trip in the woods. The cook agreed but made the mistake of wearing his moneybelt, which included his life's savings. When the two hunters were alone in the woods, the temptation of easy money overcame the greedy logger. He shot the cook to death, removed the moneybelt, dug a hole in the deep snow, and buried his companion's body. Returning to camp, he concocted a tale to account for the disappearance of the cook in the woods.

No one ever found the grave of the cook and nobody recalls the fate of Young Ryan and the moneybelt. But everyone in the Miramichi area has heard of the Dungarvon Whooper. It seems that to this day the cook's spirit protests the murder and the improper burial in the deep snow. Travellers in the area claim that at sundown they can hear horrible, eerie screams. This wailing or whooping will last ten minutes or so and then subside into silence. In the early 1900s a priest from the nearby parish at Renous performed the rite of exorcism, but the cook's spirit was too strong and reports of screams persist.

Such is the story of the Dungarvon Whooper. It is interesting to note that the Miramichi enjoyed railway service for four decades. The service ended in 1936, but not before the train was given the name The Dungarvon Whooper. As local historian Stuart Trueman noted in

Ghosts, Pirates and Treasure Trove (1975), "It was the first train in the world named in honour of a ghost."

"52 North by 21 West"

There is no tale more thrilling than the story of a rescue at sea, especially if that tale involves an element of the supernatural.

One of the most famous tales of the rescue of a ship in distress is "52 North by 21 West." It is the story of a sea rescue from Cape Breton Island and it was reported by Calum MacLeod. The captain of the ship in distress appears aboard the rescuing ship and writes the order to "Steer North by North East" on a slate.

Here is another version of that tale. This time the order for "52 North by 21 West" was given by a voice. These tales of ships being rescued are among the most dramatic of all legends, and some of them are very well documented.

The narrator of this tale is Mrs. Oswald MacMillan, who first heard it in 1912 when she lived near Murray Harbour North on the eastern end of Prince Edward Island. She later moved to Nova Scotia, where Helen Creighton recorded it.

Sometime in the 1870s, when the Earl of Dufferin was governor-general of Canada, a ship was built in Quebec and christened in honour of his wife, the Countess of Dufferin. The vessel's first few trips were uneventful. Then she went to Saint John and loaded with lumber and deals for Londonderry, Ireland, starting forth, strangely enough, on Christmas Day. Perhaps this was to take advantage of the weather, for the sea was smooth, the wind fair, and the sun shone from a cloudless sky, an unusually fine day for that time of year. This fair weather, however, was not to last, and a few days later they ran into a tremendous hurricane. This continued for two days. The wind changed then and made crossed seas so that she was dismasted.

They jettisoned their deckload of deals, but they could not prevent the raging seas from sweeping over the rails and getting into their food and water. Even the apple barrels, their last hope, were taken from them when an unexpected wave swept them overboard. In their extremity the captain told the crew that they would not drown, but they might starve since they had been swept far off their usual course and were not likely to be rescued. At that time they had no means of communicating their plight; no human means, that is. The captain said there was nothing left for them to do but pray.

We may suppose that accounts for what happened next, but we must now turn to another ship.

About the time the *Countess of Dufferin* left Saint John, the *Arlington*, a vessel built in Yarmouth, Nova Scotia, and skippered by Captain Davis of that port, set sail from Liverpool, England, for New York. As she too was favoured with fine weather, which held, there was every probability of a record trip. After they had been to sea for a week the second mate was startled one evening when Captain Davis suddenly appeared on deck like "a crazy man" and shouted to the man at the wheel, "Luff luff, quick; hail of distress."

The mate looked at him in astonishment. "Captain Davis," he said, "What's the matter?" The captain looked at him in amazement. "Didn't you hear the hail of distress?" he asked. The mate assured him he hadn't so they turned then to the wheelsman but he hadn't heard it either, nor had either of them seen anything unusual to account for it.

Supposing the captain had been resting, the mate made the obvious remark, "You were dreaming."

The captain was indignant and said with no hesitation, "I was not dreaming, I was wide awake." He fell silent for a moment and then added, "The strange part of it is that whoever called for help also gave the course we should take. It was 52 north by 21 west." The men watched him anxiously and began to feel uncomfortable. The mate knew that his captain was a stern man who took advice from no one, yet he could not keep from saying, "That's three days' sail from here."

The captain paid no attention and gave the wheelsman a change of course. Now they were really afraid and recalled that another Yarmouth captain had recently gone insane at sea. They dared not disobey, and the wheelsman followed his new directions.

Before long they too reached turbulent waters and these worsened as they sailed along. There was little sleep for the uneasy crew, for they had no idea what to expect. On the third night the captain doubled the lookouts and again the order was obeyed but not relished. The captain paced the deck, well aware that he was being observed closely. There was no sound but the wind in the rigging and the black ocean roaring past.

Then at two a.m. the lookout cried that there was something on their lee. "Can we clear it?" the captain called. The lookout said they could, and a moment later identified the object as a vessel without lights, the worst thing to be encountered upon the sea at night. As soon as they were close enough to be heard, Captain Davis clasped his megaphone and shouted, "Who are you, and why haven't you got your lights up?"

The answer came back swiftly in a tone of great relief, "We're the *Countess of Dufferin* out of Saint John. We're water-logged and we have nothing to put lights up with. Will you stand by and take us off?"

Officers and crew were speechless. Not so Captain Davis, who said matter-of-factly, and perhaps with a touch of I-told-you-so in his voice, "Certainly we'll stand by and take you off; that's what we came for." Having made himself clear, and leaving orders with his crew for the night, he went below to sleep.

When daybreak came the seas were still high but the rescue was effected. The last one to step over the *Arlington's* rail from the stricken ship was of course the captain and at that precise moment the sun came out and they were able to take their position. Officers and crew looked at Captain Davis with a new respect, for they were exactly 52 north and 21 west, the very spot where the voice had directed them.

The Female Phantom of Gagetown

A female phantom is said to inhabit the Jenkins House in the village of Gagetown on the Saint John River in New Brunswick. The two-and-a-half-storey residence with its four chimneys was built in 1810 in a pastoral setting by its original owner, the Honourable Hugh Johnson. It was acquired in the 1970s by the well-known weaver and tartan designer Patricia Jenkins.

On more than one occasion Jenkins has felt a "presence" in one of the upstairs bedrooms and in the main rooms of the house. The "presence" seemed to move from room to room. Visitors to the house felt it, not to mention the Jenkins' cat, which swivelled its head as if watching the slow progress of what has been called the Female Phantom of Gagetown.

The house has known its share of tragedies. Hugh Johnson's eldest daughter married an Englishman and died here in childbirth. One of the sons of his *fiancée* drowned in the river. One of Johnson's own sons, also engaged to be married, broke off the engagement at the last moment because he had fallen in love with his *fiancée's* younger sister. Some time after their wedding, the older sister was invited to move into the mansion with the married couple. She accepted but then found she could not stand seeing her sister in her former sweetheart's arms. She hanged herself in the closet of an upstairs bedroom.

Well before Jenkins acquired the house, but well after these tragic occurrences, twelve-year-old Peggy Lucas was an overnight guest in the house. She was sound asleep in one of the upstairs bedrooms when she awoke with a start. "I awakened just as a lady in white walked slowly from the direction of the closet right past my bed, toward the window. Her hair was down around her shoulders. I saw her plainly." The terrified young girl cried out but there was no answer. Then the lady in white vanished before her eyes.

Christ Church Ghost

Christ Church Cathedral is one of the finest examples of decorated Gothic architecture in North America. It was constructed in 1845-52, the first new cathedral erected on new foundations on British soil since the Norman Conquest of 1066. It remains the pride of Fredericton, capital of New Brunswick.

The man who caused the Cathedral to be raised was the Right Reverend John Medley, first Anglican bishop of Fredericton, a man greatly concerned with religious music and church architecture. He died on September 9, 1892, and his body rests in the marble tomb at the end of the north aisle.

The Cathedral has many points of interest; one of the most interesting is the identity of the ghost of the Cathedral. Surprisingly, it is not the ghost of Bishop Medley that has been seen, but the spirit of his second wife, Margaret Hudson Medley, who survived him in life and even in death. It is said that to this day Mrs. Medley's ghostly form may be seen making its way from the old Dr. Crockett home on Queen Street, gliding along Church Street, and entering the west door of the Cathedral. There the restless spirit surveys the magnificence of the Cathedral, as if in wonderment, and then simply disappears.

Reports of the apparition of Mrs. Medley go back for a century. In all accounts, she is seen, as she was in life, as a stately and reserved woman, wearing white. Sightings are sometimes reported on September 9, the anniversary of the death of William the Conqueror, but also that of the death of the Right Reverend John Medley.

The Rowing Man

Generations of collectors of dulse, the edible purple seaweed, report that on some moonlit nights, above the sound of the sea, they hear the sound of rowing. When they look up from their dulse collecting, they can see the apparition of an older man in a dory some distance out. The Rowing Man appears for a minute or two, slowly rowing by. Then he and his dory vanish in the night.

The apparition of the Rowing Man generally appears on the night of November 19, and again on the night of November 25. No one has any idea who he is supposed to be or the nature of his mission. The phantom figure is simply known as the Rowing Man of Little Dark Harbour.

Little Dark Harbour lies on the west coast of the island of Grand Manan, New Brunswick. It is well named, being a somewhat "dark" place, rocky and uncharacteristically bleak. The rest of Grand Manan Island has been called the "Bermuda of the Maritimes."

Vision of a Newly Dead Friend

During the early years of the Second World War, P.K. Page was in her mid-twenties and living in a house that was neither old nor new in the town of Rothesay, New Brunswick. She was alone in her room one evening, grieving the loss of a close friend. Then the close friend appeared....

Page went on to write brilliant poems, but she never could forget or account for the vision. In June 1987, she recalled her feelings and sensations at the time.

I had loved her dearly, and hers was my first death. During our years of friendship, we had talked about many things, including the possibility of life after death. I suggested that it might be possible; she took the other view. But neither of us had strong opinions on the matter. After all, we didn't know.

Then before me in the room I saw a curious, molecular dance. I stared at it and it began to look like a Morse code printed on the air. Then it densened, and became the very real shape of my friend. She looked radiant and extraordinarily beautiful.

"So I was right after all," I said, overjoyed.

"Yes," she replied. "That's why I came back — to tell you."

"Then, what is it like? Tell me — what is dying like?"

"Every death is personal. My death is of no use to you. But there is nothing to grieve about." And I believed her.

That is all we said. We smiled at each other, placed our fingers on each other's arms, the beginning of an embrace. I could feel her flesh with my fingertips. Then I felt it disintegrate, like uncooked rice. I pulled back and again I saw a molecular dance, a swarm of midges in the air, and then nothing.

The interesting thing is that since that evening I never have grieved for her. I have missed her, of course, and still do, but since that evening I know there is nothing to grieve about.

The Little Man

The Little Man is the terror of the motorist.

The apparition is that of a tubby little man who wears a flat-topped hat. He appears only on foggy nights. He darts out of the woods and races alongside the speeding automobile. Then he overtakes the vehicle, and to the horror of the driver, throws himself in front of the car. The motorist slams on the brakes and brings the car to an abrupt halt. But there is no impact, no collision. When the motorist gets out of the car and looks around, there is no trace of the Little Man.

This hair-raising phenomenon is said to take place on the few kilometres of lonely roadway that link Dark Harbour to the north with Ghost Hollow to the south on Grand Manan Island, New Brunswick.

Another version of the Little Man is the Flying Spectre, a white-robed woman, her hands held out ahead of her as if in supplication, her blonde hair streaming well behind her. Stepping out of the woods, she leaps in front of speeding automobiles on one of the lonely stretches of highway between Richibucto and Rexton.

Motorists, beware!

The Prophet's Room

There is a tradition on the campus of Acadia University in Wolfville, Nova Scotia, that the Prophet's Room is haunted. The Prophet's Room is not really a single room but a small suite of rooms located in the Women's Residence, a gracious, classical-style edifice erected in 1879, the oldest building on campus. They are for the use of visiting lecturers.

One visiting lecturer was Alexandre L. Amprimoz, who arrived from Brock University in St. Catharines, Ontario, where he teaches the Romance languages. He was assigned the suite, and at the time he had no knowledge of the local tradition that the rooms were haunted. Here is how he described his first night in the suite:

In September of 1984, during a lecture tour of the Maritimes, I was given the Prophet's Room where I stayed three nights. I had not been told that the building was haunted by the ghost of a young woman who had hanged herself there several years ago.

The first night I suddenly awoke and saw that the windows were opened and a light wind moved the curtains. I saw a young blonde woman combing her hair at the dresser. She was semi-transparent. I closed my eyes and hid under the sheets. I could hear noises, pacing, but a few minutes later all returned to silence.

Today members of the faculty cannot recall why this particular suite is known as the Prophet's Room. Perhaps it should be called the Spirit's Room.

The UPEI Haunting

The University of Prince Edward Island is a pleasant place to study, but the university is too young to have ghosts of its own. Or is it?

David K. MacKinnon of Charlottetown had a strange experience there as an undergraduate. He wrote about it in a dispatch posted to the Internet. I am pleased to reproduce it in his own words:

During my time at the University of Prince Edward Island, I have heard of a number of campus hauntings. As background, our campus used to be two campuses, St. Dunstan's University and Prince of Wales College. The two amalgamated in the late 1960s (1968 I believe) to form the only university in this province.

The first haunting dates back to when the building currently in use by the Home Economics department was used as a male residence. On this particular night, two students were in the town having a high old time. A snowstorm began to blow up and they started back. One was slower than the other, so he asked his friend to go on ahead and make sure the door was open because he knew he would not make it back before curfew when the front door would be locked. The friend went on ahead and made it just before the door was locked, but he was banished to his room for being so late.

Later, the second room-mate arrived to find the door locked and no way to get in. He pounded on the door, but the priests would not let him in, intending to teach him a lesson. An hour or so later, the first room-mate, worried for his friend, heard a knock at the dorm room door. He went up to answer it, sure it was his room-mate, but all that greeted him was a cold draft of air. He looked down to see a trail of water leading to the staircase from his doorway. Puzzled, he returned to bed. The next morning, the second room-mate was found frozen to death outside the front door.

Ever since that night, staff or students who are working late in the building during a particularly blustery winter's night may find a cold breeze blow past them and look down to see the same trail of water leading from a particular room to the staircase. Such is the tale of Dalton Hall.

The next haunting is a more uplifting story surrounding the

Cass Chemistry Building. Father Cass was a benevolent soul and a caring teacher during the early part of the century. When he died, the building was named in his honour as he had spent most of his life teaching chemistry to the college's varied population. It is said that Father Cass still roams the halls, looking after his students, even those who were born long after his death.

One night, two chemistry students were working late on a project. Despite the rule that no one is allowed to work alone in the building in case something happens, one student decided to make a quick run down to the local Burger King for something to tide them over through the wee hours. The second student was left on the top floor to look after the experiment.

Not long after the first student left, the second heard a noise from downstairs. Thinking it might be his/her partner, they went downstairs to see who was there. Before I go any farther, you must understand that there is one staircase inside the building, thus one way from the main level to the top. The fire escape is accessible from the second floor and up, but has never been used due to its advanced state of disrepair. There would be no way for a person to get through the building without being seen or heard. Also consider that sound travels very well in this empty building at night.

To return to the story, they went downstairs to see who it was. Not finding anyone, nor hearing anyone in the building, they went back upstairs. There they found the Bunsen burner that had been left burning was shut off, the gas shut down both at the nozzle and the wall, and the tube neatly rolled up. It was then that this student remembered the stories of Father Cass putting things away that were left unattended.

There is only one other historic haunting I can think of, but we refuted it with a bit of investigation. Apparently in the Main Building, before it was renovated, a certain room would be seen from the outside to have a light on. Not so strange you say, but if you look closely you can see a figure hanging from the ceiling. Apparently, one of the professors had hanged himself in that room. Ever since then, the room could be seen from the outside to be lit, revealing a dim figure swinging slowly on the end of a rope from the ceiling. If you tried to find the room, you would find the only door into it covered with boxes. Remove the boxes and unlock the door and you would find an empty light socket.

As I said, we disproved this. There was another way into the room.

The last story I will relate is a bit hard for me to believe, even though I was there. I am a skeptic by nature. I believe there probably is more to this world than meets the eye. Psychic powers may be possible, though I see precognition as being incredibly perceptive and being able to deduce the future based on a paranormal knowledge of what is happening in the world (beyond normal human perception, that is).

It has been said by the women of Bernadine Hall, the campus's women's residence, that the lounge on the fourth floor is a focus for spirits. Of this I'm skeptical, but I have an open mind so I'll reserve my disbelief until I see proof either way.

On one particular night we decided to try a seance using the Ouija board. Now, I have been described as being an excellent receiver, one of the reasons they wanted me involved. Once I was asked to try to describe a house as a friend of mine "walked" through it in his mind. I was able to describe the house in detail, down to the colour and style of furniture and the geodesic dome in the backyard. I've not been able to explain it, but I haven't seen the place either. I'll reserve my judgement of what I saw until then.

Back to the story. Several of us took part in this, taking turns (male with female) on the board to see if we could find anything. Soon, we started feeling cold, and one of the more sensitive of the group began to take on a different personality. Now, we were all trying to be open to spirits. I was trying my hand at automatic writing as this was happening. The person affected was at the Ouija board. He began to talk as if he were a scared young girl. At the same time, I and another friend got this incredibly clear vision of a room in this building, but we could feel it was on the other side of the building on the third floor. My vision was of looking out over a bed from a black room to an open doorway.

Standing in the doorway was a young woman wearing a skirt to just below the knee and shoulder-length hair. The light from the hallway was shining in behind her. I could feel fear of ... the girl? Something, anyway ... and a feeling that I had to get past her into the light. At the same time, one of the women had a vision of looking onto a dark room on the opposite side of the building at a young woman cowering behind a bed. The feeling she received was of concern for the girl, who looked to be terrified, but of what she didn't know.

These stories were heard by an independent witness so we would not trade information, so I'm at a loss to explain it. Was it a vision of a person cowering in fear, or did we simply have a psychically linked dream? Or did the independent witness collaborate with my friend to match her story to mine? I guess I'll never know.

By the way, the person who became "possessed" was faking it. Or at least he appeared to be faking.

QUEBEC

The Talking Head

From the days of Ville-Marie comes the strange story of the Talking Head.

Jean de Saint-Père (1618-1657) was a Frenchman who became a colonist in New France to assist in the conversion of the Iroquois. He was a pious person and he must have been a responsible man because he served as the first clerk of the court and the first notary in the colony of Ville-Marie, today's Montreal. Sieur de Maisonneuve thought so much of the notary that when he signed Saint-Père's marriage contract, he included a generous grant of land "to reward him for his good and faithful services."

Saint-Père came to a tragic end on October 25, 1657. He was only thirty-nine at the time. It seems that while constructing a house, he received a group of Iroquois. Apparently without warning they turned on him, killing him and cutting off his head. They did so, apparently, to possess his fine growth of hair.

As they were fleeing with their trophy, Saint-Père's decapitated head began to speak. It spoke in very good Iroquois, a language Saint-Père had never learned during his life. It reproached the Indians for their faithlessness: "You kill us, you inflict endless cruelties on us, you want to annihilate the French, you will not succeed, they will one day be your masters and you will obey them."

Once it started to speak, the Talking Head would not stop reprimanding the Iroquois. One can imagine the consternation and fright of the warriors. They tried to silence it by leaving it behind them, by covering it, by burying it, but to no avail. The avenging voice continued to make itself heard. At long last they scalped the head and disposed of it, keeping the head of hair as a trophy of victory. Yet the Iroquois heard the voice of Saint-Père. It whispered from its hair.

The Talking Head became a tradition among the Oneida Indians of the Iroquois Confederacy.

The Quebec Werewolf

On Halloween nights, television stations will schedule a feast of horror movies, and sometimes they include a revival of *The Wolf Man*, the classic horror movie produced by Universal Pictures. It stars Lon Chaney, Jr., as Lawrence Talbot, the young man who is doomed to turn into a wolf at the time of the full moon.

A werewolf is a human being who turns into a wolf and back again. The French equivalent is the *loup-garou*. The werewolf feeds on human beings. Lycanthropy is the technical name for this "taste." Wolves are frightening enough without the superstitious fear that their bodies harbour the souls of doomed men!

Here is an account that appeared in English in the *Quebec Gazette*, December 10, 1764.

* ⊷⊷◦⊶◦⊷◦⊷⊷ *

Intelligence Extraordinary

Kamouraska, Dec. 2. We learn that a *Ware-Wolfe*, which has roamed through this Province for several Years, and done great Destruction in the District of Quebec, has received several considerable Attacks in the Month of October last, by different Animals, which they had armed and incensed against this Monster; and especially, the 3d of November following, he received such a furious Blow, from a small lean Beast, that it was thought they were entirely delivered from this fatal Animal, as it some Time after retired into its Hole, to the great Satisfaction of the Public. But they have just learn'd, as the most surest Misfortune, that this Beast is not entirely destroyed, but begins again to show itself, more furious than ever, and makes terrible Hovock wherever it goes. — *Beware then of the Wiles of this malicious Beast, and take good Care of falling into its Claws.*

The Hudson Poltergeist

The village of Hudson on the Ottawa River was much in the news in October 1880, when poltergeist-like activity at the Hudson Hotel, owned by innkeeper John Park, attracted onlookers from far and wide.

Manifestations began in a small way in mid-September of that year, and a curious fact was that the disturbances at the hotel occurred not at night but during the day.

On Friday, October 1, 1880, the innkeeper was summoned to examine some unlet rooms where the beds had been tossed about. Mattresses, chairs, tables, sheets, and blankets had been scattered about and mixed. Pillows were tied together to represent someone sitting on a chair. Some unseen agent had opened the windows and doors, all carefully shut the day before.

The disturbances were not limited to the unrented rooms. In the kitchen, the cook was cutting a loaf of bread. She left the loaf on the table and went into the next room for a few minutes. When she returned, the loaf was unaccountably missing. She searched high and low for it, and it was eventually found in the clothes-basket in the adjoining room.

Some of these manifestations occurred in the presence of neighbours who were attracted by reports of odd happenings at the hotel. Then they took a serious turn. At eleven o'clock on Saturday morning, a fire broke out in the hayloft of the stables. Only with difficulty was the spread of the fire limited to the stables.

Later that day the *curé* of the local parish was summoned. He prayed and sprinkled holy water, and while things were quiet as long as the priest was in attendance, no sooner had he left that there was a resumption of the disturbances. Bottles of liquor in the tavern began to move about of their own accord. There was more mayhem in the bedrooms.

Another priest was summoned on Sunday, October 3, and about one hundred onlookers, some from Oka across the river, observed him as he sprinkled holy water and performed the rite of exorcism. It seemed to work, for there was no resumption of manifestations. There were no further reports of poltergeist-like activity at the Hudson Hotel. No reason was ever given for the activity and no one was ever blamed or even suspected of causing the mayhem or setting the fire.

Another Hudson Poltergeist

The year following the disturbances at the Hudson Hotel, the village of Hudson on the Ottawa River was the scene of further poltergeist-like activity. This time the poltergeist struck at the home of a Mme. Perrault.

On Saturday, May 14, 1881, the disturbances began. A reporter for the *Montreal Star* who had travelled from Montreal to Hudson described the domestic scene: "On a bureau in the small sitting room were twelve statuettes or religious figures in porcelain, set in two concentric horseshoes, six in each. These were all found lying on their faces. They were set up. A little later they were found lying on their backs. Set up again. The third time they were found on their sides. Set up once more. The fourth time the heads were all put together as in the centre of the circle, and the feet laid out symmetrically as so many spokes of a wheel." No one saw anyone moving the statues. The sitting room was empty at the time.

There were four days of peace before the manifestations resumed: "A small table in the bedroom, which stood at an oblique angle from the wall, was set at right angles, then tilted on two legs against the bed, and one pillow and the counterpane were drawn over it." That was only the beginning. Strange things happened each day. "Two little winding sheets, which had been stowed away in a valise, were laid out on the bed, as if to answer their original purpose. A woman's shawl hanging upon the frame of a door was thrown upon the bed. A cupboard standing at the foot of the bed was set ajar, and a pile of napkins and towels placed on the foot of the bed without being folded. A prayer book was wafted from the sitting room to the foot of this same bed. A little toy stove on top of a bureau was toppled over and a photograph leaning against the wall was thrown forward."

Mme. Perrault, thirty-five years old and the mother of five children, lived in the house with her mother and grandmother. She said the disturbances proceeded without noise. Only once, it seems, had she heard a noise, and that was when a wicker chair in the sitting-room was thrown over. There were further disturbances in the upstairs bedrooms. "Dresses hung up on pegs along the walls were taken down and stretched on the floor. The same with under-clothing, drawers, etc. Mme. Perrault's best Sunday dress received special attention in this way. A roll of lace on a small table was nicely unrolled on the bed. One of the two windows of the garret opened spontaneously. In the kitchen four willow chairs were placed back to back and a buffalo robe was spread over them. That same robe was unhung from the wall and spread over a cart." The reporter saw this when he arrived on the scene. "He also saw where two pillows had been put together and a quilt which was lightly tucked under the bedding had been rolled over them, making the figure look like a corpse laid out."

No one had observed any of this happening. No one had any idea why this was happening. "God only knows," Mme. Perrault said, when asked the cause. "My husband is working on the Intercolonial at Rivière du Loup, and we thought at first he was dead and that it was his spirit returning to us." A telegraph operator ascertained that this was not so.

The reporter, on leaving the house, passed a thirteen-year-old girl "whose eyes were queer, and who had twitching of the arms and facial features." Before boarding the train to Montreal, he paid a visit to the Abbé Hurteau, *curé* of the parish. "He was well-received by that gentleman, and while the two were exchanging views in the garden, a horseman rode up in haste, and informed His Reverence that the young girl in question, named Ernestine Perrault, had, immediately on our departure, been taken with convulsions and that it took two men to hold her. His Reverence then decided to make a thorough investigation into the circumstances connected with the mystery, particularly as to the little girl, and the reporter sat down to await developments."

The *curé* found Ernestine was reluctant to meet him, and when she agreed, he found her shy and surprised that anyone would suspect her of causing the disturbances. "She is full grown for her age, a brunette with elongated face and bright eyes, and her form is as lithe as a willow," wrote the reporter. She was newly subject to convulsions. She remembered nothing of what had happened during her convulsions. Then she had a fit and showed that she was able to perform feats of endurance. "She thrust her hand through a large pane of glass, splintering it to atoms, without making the slightest scratch on the skin or drawing a globule of blood." The fit lasted about an hour.

The reporter interviewed the villagers and noted a local tradition. The gossip was that a curse had been placed on the Perrault household and this is the cause of the problems. "It appears that it is an old hag wandering up and down the ranges, in quest of charity, who threw a spell upon the house and girl. The reason she gives, in the forges and barnyards where she tarries, is that her husband worked for Perrault, and in settling accounts there was a balance of $4.00 due him, which has never been paid." The villagers seemed to feel that the disturbances were "small potatoes" because the old hag was capable of real harm:

causing the house to be overrun with rats, for instance. It was felt that the problems were caused by Satan.

He wrote, "'So long as that money is not paid, let them look out,' saith Meg Merrilies, pointing her bony finger up the road."

Then, on Monday, the *curé* visited the house of Mme. Perrault. He ordered everyone in the house outdoors to see for himself that there was no fraud. He arranged the bedding and chairs and closed the room so that no one could get in, and sometime after when he returned into the room the bedding was tossed and the chairs moved from where he placed them. "I am also informed that the girl (the supposed medium) on coming home from school noticed one of the attic windows open, which was not usual, and she asked her mother why the window was open and her mother said that the windows were not open, at the same time going upstairs to make sure, when to her surprise the window was open and the door was covered with clothing, scattered about every way."

So it was never established that Ernestine had actually caused the disturbances, but it was suspected she was the focus of the poltergeist-like action.

The Walling-in of Peggy Green

Quebec's Eastern Townships are full of interesting stories. Some of them are accounts of ghosts. One such story, backed by rock-hard evidence, is that of the Walling-in of Peggy Green.

Travellers on the Old Mexico Road in the vicinity of Island-Brook, east of Cookshire, will pass the Irish cemetery. There they will see that one of the low mounds of the cemetery has been walled-in. Local inhabitants identify the walled-in area as the burial-place of Peggy Green.

In the 1880s, farmers found that entire herds of their cows were yielding no milk. They laid a trap, caught a large white rabbit, and notched its ears before setting it free. Shortly thereafter an old Roman Catholic Irish farmer's wife named Peggy Green died. It was noted that her ears were notched in the manner of the rabbit's. She was buried in the Irish cemetery but the curse did not lift. The cows still did not give milk. So the farmers walled-in her burial-place to "contain" her ghost. The stones did the job and the cows began to produce normally.

The u-shaped, walled-in area may be seen to this day. Old-timers shun the cemetery by night. But then it is commonly believed by the old-timers of this part of the Eastern Townships that if on the night of a full moon you take the bones of a black chicken to the crossroads you will see the devil!

The Dagg Poltergeist

The Dagg Poltergeist was one of the wonders of the Ottawa Valley in the late nineteenth century. The focus of the disturbances caused by the poltergeist (an unseen but noisy spirit) was the farmhouse of George and Susan Dagg in the village of Clarendon on the north side of the Ottawa River, near Shawville, Quebec. The Daggs were a typical farming family. They had two children of their own, four-year-old Susan and two-year-old John. The family was increased by one member when they adopted Dinah Burden McLean, an eleven-year-old Scottish orphan.

John Dagg and sixteen of his fellow farmers described some of the manifestations that took place on his farm in a short Report that was prepared by them at the request of Percy Woodcock, a journalist who covered the exciting events for the *Brockville Recorder and Times*. The manifestations extended over a period of about three months. The events were observed by Woodcock and by the witnesses who signed this statement, as well as by numerous spectators who were attracted to the little community from far and wide by reports of wondrous happenings. So close was Woodcock to the action, that many observers (especially rival reporters and correspondents) felt that he was somehow orchestrating it.

R.S. Lambert devoted a chapter to the Dagg Poltergeist in *Exploring the Supernatural* (1955). He called his account "The Ghost that Talked." The chapter concludes with these words:

Most readers of this chapter will feel inclined to set the affair down to fraud, or hallucination. If so, one would like to know the answers to a few supplementary questions. What benefit did the Daggs, or the girl Dinah, get out of it? If it was a mere case of hysterical exhibitionism, why did it suddenly stop in the early hours of November 18th, and never repeat itself? What degree of skill in ventriloquism was necessary to trick such a large crowd of people? Did Dinah (if she was the agent) ever display such skill in later life?

Alas, to these questions history gives us no answer!

Report

To whom it may concern:

We, the undersigned, solemnly declare that the following curious proceedings, which began on the 15th day of September, 1889, and are still going on, on the 17th day of November, 1889, in the home of Mr. George Dagg, a farmer living seven miles from Shawville, Clarendon Township, Pontiac County, Province of Quebec, actually occurred as below described.

1st, That fires have broken out spontaneously through the house, as many as eight occurring on one day, six being in the house and two outside; that the window curtains were burned whilst on the windows, this happening in broad daylight whilst the family and neighbours were in the house.

2nd, That stones were thrown by invisible hands through the windows, as many as eight panes of glass being broken; that articles such as waterjug, milk pitcher, a wash basin, cream jug, butter tub and other articles were thrown about the house by the same invisible agency; a jar of water being thrown in the face of Mrs. John Dagg, also in the face of Mrs. George Dagg, whilst they were busy about their household duties, Mrs. George Dagg being alone in the house at the time it was thrown in her face; that a large shelf was heard distinctly to be played and was seen to move across the room on to the floor; immediately after, a rocking chair began rocking furiously. That a washboard was sent flying down the stairs from the garret, no one being in the garret at the time. That when the child Dinah is present, a deep gruff voice like that of an aged man has been heard at various times, both in the house and outdoors, and when asked questions answered so as to be distinctly heard, showing that he is cognizant of all that has taken place, not only in Mr. Dagg's family but also in the families of the surrounding neighbourhood. That he claims to be a discarnated being who died twenty years ago, aged eighty years; that he gave his name to Mr. George Dagg and to Mr. Willie Dagg, forbidding them to tell it. That this intelligence is able to make himself visible to Dinah, little Mary and Johnnie, who have seen him under different forms at different times, at one time as a tall thin man with a cow's head, horns and cloven foot, at another time as a big black dog, and finally as a man with a beautiful face and long white hair, dressed in white, wearing a crown with stars in it.

John Dagg, Portage du Fort, P.Q.; George Dagg, Portage du Fort, P.Q.; William Eddes, Radsford, P.Q.; William H. Dagg, Port. du Fort; Arthur Smart, Port. du Fort; Charles A. Dagg, Port. du Fort; Bruno Morrow, Port. du Fort; Benjamin Smart, Shawville, P.Q.; William J. Dagg, Shawville, P.Q.; Robert J. Peever, Cobden, Ont.; Robert H. Lockhart, Port. du Fort; John Fulford, Port. du Fort; George H. Hodgins, Shawville; Richard E. Dagg, Shawville; George Blackwell, Haley's, Ont.; William Smart, Portage du Fort; John J. Dagg, Portage du Fort.

Dr. Brunelle's Crisis Apparition

A crisis apparition is the appearance of a close friend or loved one at the time of his or her death in another part of the world.

Dr. J.A.F. Brunelle was a prominent general physician in Montreal. On December 28, 1897, he was sitting in the office of his house at 698 Sherbrooke Street. It was Sunday, so he was relaxing, reading a book. There was a knock on the door. Thinking it was his son, he did not look up, but he inquired what he wanted. To his surprise he received no reply. There was another knock on the door. He looked up and was amazed to see standing before him Dr. Treffle Garceau, an old friend who lived in Boston.

Brunelle asked, "How did you get into the house?" He had heard two sets of knocks but no one had rung the doorbell. There was no reply, so he rose to his feet to shake hands with his friend, but as he did so, the visitor seemed to fade from his sight.

Brunelle looked everywhere, but could find no trace of his old friend. He gave a loud exclamation of surprise.

Mme. Brunelle, who had been in another part of the house, entered and inquired what was the matter. Brunelle answered evasively and asked to be left alone.

He was still pondering the mystery half an hour later, when the telephone rang and he received the message that Dr. Treffle Garceau had just died in Boston. Brunelle was astounded, but was loathe to make the matter public. He told only a few close friends. The story spread abroad, however, and created quite a sensation, especially among the spiritualists, who were numerous in Montreal at the time. It attracted national press coverage.

As one reporter wrote, "When questioned, Brunelle submitted the story and said his explanation, which appeared to be most natural, that it was some kind of supernatural intervention. He did not formerly believe in apparitions but cannot refuse to believe that Providence is able to act in that way and to employ those means to make him believe in that kind of phenomena. Dr. Garceau, who studied medicine here, practised over thirty years in Boston and paid particular attention to the religious community and the poor. He was a brother-in-law of L.O. David, the city clerk, and a great friend of Louis Frechette, the well-known writer."

Did Dr. Brunelle "see" Dr. Garceau? Did the latter "visit" the former at the time of his death? Perhaps to say goodbye?

A Singular Case

This case of poltergeistery comes from the free-flowing pen of Sir Arthur Conan Doyle. In his later years the creator of Sherlock Holmes travelled throughout the English-speaking world espousing the cause of "spirit return" and "spirit communication." In 1922, he delivered two lectures on

Spiritualism to full houses and described the experience in *Our Second American Adventure* (1924).

A singular case of *poltergeist* haunting came under my notice whilst at Montreal. It had occurred to a couple, the man an experienced journalist, the wife a rather nervous lady of middle age. They lived alone, their only child having gone out into the world. These people were haunted by a very active and mischievous but at the same time harmless spirit or spirits. The box of bricks that had been their child's toy was dragged out and fantastic buildings erected, which were put up again as soon as dismantled. When one of these buildings was photographed, a queer little mannikin figure came out in the photograph behind the bricks, and beside it what looks like a female head. There seemed to be two haunters, for presently direct writing began to appear upon pieces of paper scattered over the house. I examined these and found distinctly two scripts, one of a grown-up person and the other of a child, which corresponded with the photograph. A picture of a house was also drawn, an extraordinary high, thin erection of twelve stories, with "the Middlesex House" written underneath. It was very well drawn. Occasionally the pranks were of a less harmless nature. The electric lights were switched off at untoward moments, and the pictures were stripped from the walls. Twice the husband was assaulted by pillows until his incredibility had been buffeted out of him. Prayer seemed of no avail. Unhappily it seldom is in such cases. I have notes of one where a large fur hearthrug was the centre of the disturbance. A priest was brought in to exorcise the force, and whilst he was in the midst of his exorcism the rug sprang at him and enveloped his head and shoulders, so that he ran terrified from the house. One is dealing with a mischievous and rather malicious child, and reason together with kindness is the only weapon. In this particular case at Montreal the couple were finally compelled to abandon the house. The haunting seemed to be local, for it did not follow them.

Stalked by a Ghost

To be stalked is bad enough. To be stalked by "a tall man dressed in black" is even worse.

John Reynolds was "one of the old-timers" of Old Chelsea, Quebec, according to folklorist Joan Finnigan. In his youth, well before the turn of the century, he worked in the Gilmour shanties in the Maniwaki district. In later years he recalled a horrifying experience that occurred to him at the time. It sounds more like a legend than it does a true story, but Reynolds maintained it happened.

It was toward the end of the shanty season and I had started out to make my way home alone. I had to travel over a lonely stretch of road through dense forest in the dead of night in order to be on time to catch the stagecoach for Maniwaki the next morning. I had been warned against travelling that stretch of road alone at night. All sorts of weird stories were circulated, one of them having to do with a "ghost" that patrolled the road all night. But I had to meet the stagecoach, and so I set forth.

It was early evening when I left the camp. Just before dusk I came to a house on the side of the road where the occupant implored me to put up at his place for the night. However, I ignored his warnings and kept on my way. I had walked about four miles — it was pitch dark by this time — when a figure resembling a tall man dressed in black suddenly loomed up beside me.

The figure seemed to appear out of the mists. There were no footsteps or other warnings of its approach. Not a word was spoken, but the figure walked right beside me. Whenever I quickened my pace, it did likewise; if I swerved to one side of the road, it followed suit. I must admit that the chills were running up and down my spine and I was sweating. But I kept right on walking, all the time wondering what the climax of this weird experience was going to be.

After we had walked about a mile and a half, we came to an opening in the forest, and the moment we entered that opening, the ghost disappeared — vanished into thin air. Three miles farther on, I woke a man who was to row me across the Desert River. On the way over, I told him of my experience with the ghost.

"You were a very brave man," he said, "to venture forth on that piece of road alone at night. A good many years ago a man was found murdered on the side of that road and was buried where he was found. Ever since then, his ghost has haunted the ground and scared the devil out of many a good man."

The Haunting of Willow Place Inn

A ghost named Maud is reputed to haunt the Willow Place Inn at Hudson, Quebec.

The beautifully situated inn overlooks the south shore of Lac des Deux-Montagnes. It was built as a private residence in 1820 and served as a meeting place for the *Patriotes* in the Rebellion of 1837. Here the *Patriotes* hatched their plans for the uprising at Saint-Eustache, which occurred on December 14, 1837.

Maud, the servant girl, overheard their plans. Her sympathies lay with the Militia and not with the *Patriotes*, so the rebels felt they had no choice but to murder her. In the middle of the night they secretly buried her body in the mud floor of the basement of the residence. It is Maud's ghost that haunts the building to this day.

Today the former residence is run as a country inn, an attractive building of Georgian and Victorian design. The owners report that there are poltergeist-like disturbances which seem to commence "when the wind begins to blow across the Lac des Deux-Montagnes and there is snow in the air." Traditionally the haunting starts on Halloween Night and extends throughout the month of November. Then it inexplicably lets up until the following October 31.

Employees have found rocks piled up outside the door of Room 8. Mushrooms grown in the basement, above the place where Maud is said to lie buried, are found beheaded. The basement door slams shut of its own accord. Chairs are knocked over. Pretty songs are heard being sung when no one is singing, and there are those who discern in the air the perfumed presence of Maud.

La Vieille Chapelle Ramsay

La Vieille Chapelle Ramsay, or the Old Ramsay Chapel, is a guest house with a picturesque situation on the south side of the Chemin des Pères. From its promontory the Chapel overlooks the city of Magog, which stretches along the eastern shores of Lake Memphrémagog in Quebec's Eastern Townships. The lake itself is said to be the habitat of a fabulous lake monster known as Memphré. Farther along the road lies the Benedictine abbey, St-Benoît-du-Lac.

The location of the Old Ramsay Chapel is not only picturesque, but also inspired.

The guest house is a bed and breakfast establishment with an art gallery to display local arts and crafts. The establishment is owned and operated by a charming married couple with one child, Regina Makuch and Jean-Louis Le Cavalier. Regina was born in the Maritimes and is of Ukrainian and Celtic background. Jean-Louis Le Cavalier is a Quebecker from Mont-Saint-Hilaire to the north. They are well suited to the operation of La Vieille Chapelle Ramsay.

The seventeen-room Ramsay mansion with chapel dates from the period 1860-80. It was built as his home by Monsignor David Shaw Ramsay (who is identified in some history texts with a hyphen as Shaw-Ramsay). Born in Scotland, Ramsay (1827-1906) was a Presbyterian cleric who settled in Quebec, where in 1859 he converted to Catholicism. He was received into the Jesuit order in England in 1867. Ramsay returned to Quebec and was appointed Chaplain of the Montreal Prison in 1891. Six years later he became a parish priest in the Magog area, taking up full-time residence in the mansion. He died in Montreal; his remains are interred in the Cathedral of Montreal.

The main characteristic of the mansion is the large, second-storey chapel with its high ceiling. The Monsignor caused it to be built, and here he conducted both private and parish services.

The following event occurred in November 1994. Regina and Jean-Louis Le Cavalier, on the market for a house to convert to bed-and-breakfast use, were immediately attracted to the possibilities of the Ramsay mansion, but they knew nothing of its history.

Regina regards herself as a sensitive person, someone who picks up feelings, thoughts, and ambiences. In the house she felt she could hear voices. More a feeling than a sound, she sensed one voice in particular, one sound more than any other. It was a sobbing sound. She delved into the history of the house. When she learned about the Monsignor, she felt he was communicating with her. A short while later she experienced visions, seeing the Monsignor's face, sensing that he wanted his chapel restored as a place for Christians to meditate, where people could find answers to their questions. The voices and the vision stressed that the work of restoration should begin in earnest, and that once the chapel was restored, people would flock there. Work on the chapel and the three guest rooms was completed on January 12, 1995, when La Vieille Chapelle Ramsay was opened. Business has been brisk.

There are three guest rooms, and each has its own motif: dolphins, doves, deer. The lounge has a snowy owl in flight. Akella, the wolf, dominates the hallway. The wall murals are the work of the artist Geneviève Reesör.

The walls of the chapel were freshly plastered and the wood was reworked. Local artist Erik Léo Trudel was commissioned to decorate the chapel, painting the walls and ceiling sky blue and adding baroque figures, including the black-robed Monsignor holding a happy baby in his arms and a baroque orchestra of angels. One angel, who is strumming the harp, has Regina's face; another angel is recognizably Jean-Louis. An art historian might describe the work as faux-folk, rather in the work of Louis de Niverville. The chapel is most inviting.

The uniqueness of the Old Ramsay Chapel is a testimony to the hard work of Regina and Jean-Louis, as well as to the power of vision.

ONTARIO

The Baldoon Mystery

The earliest and eeriest haunting in the history of Upper Canada (as early Ontario was known) is the Baldoon Mystery.

The haunting took place in a farmhouse in the ill-fated colony of Baldoon. The colony was established in 1804, when Lord Selkirk resettled over one hundred dispossessed Highland Scots on the swampy land on the north shore of Lake St. Clair, between the present-day cities of Wallaceburg and Chatham. He held out hope that the frugal but hard-working Scots would become prosperous sheep farmers. But the settlement fell into decline and the settlers dispersed even before the War of 1812 dealt it a deathblow. Thus did Baldoon become a ghost colony.

Today an official plaque marks the site of the historic Baldoon Settlement. But its inscription makes no mention of the Baldoon Mystery, the sole event of continuing interest in the short history of Lord Selkirk's ill-conceived colonization scheme.

What happened at Baldoon was this. The large frame farmhouse of John McDonald and his family became the focus of a three-year haunting by a poltergeist. The haunting took place between the years 1829 and 1831. Over this period curiosity-seekers came from far and wide to witness the strange and inexplicable events. No ghosts were ever seen but dozens of witnesses reported hearing, seeing, and feeling typical poltergeist disturbances: hails of bullets, stones, and lead pellets; water and fire descending upon the house as if from the heavens. No one was ever hurt, yet on at least one occasion the house heaved from its foundations. The disturbances ended only with the house catching fire and burning to the ground.

Was the McDonald farmhouse being haunted by the Devil? Was the cause of the commotion a poltergeist, or "noisy spirit"? Students of such matters point out that the Baldoon Mystery follows the worldwide poltergeist pattern, right down to the fact that the McDonald family included a pubescent girl whose name was Dinah. Skeptics have always maintained that the disturbances were, pure and simple, the product of hysteria, gossip, fear, superstition, and possibly revenge.

Whatever the cause or causes of the disturbances, there were many witnesses to the eerie events that took place at the McDonald farmhouse.

Close to forty years after the disturbances, Neil T. McDonald, the younger son of the original owner, returned to the community where he was able to locate twenty-six of the older residents. They were willing to speak to him and he collected their statements and published them serially in the *Wallaceburg News*. The testimonials were then collected and printed in the form of a booklet entitled *The Baldoon Mysteries*.

One of the witnesses was William S. Fleury, an original member of the community whose farmhouse was just up the road from the McDonalds'. Here is what he had to say about the Baldoon Mystery:

It was rumoured that there was a great mystery going on at McDonald's, and I, like a great many others, went to see for myself. I saw stones and brick bats coming through the doors and windows, making the hole whatever size the article was that came in. Parties would take these same things and throw them into the river, and in a few minutes they would come back again. I saw a child lying in a little cradle, when the cradle began to rock fearfully and no one was near it. They thought it would throw the child out, so two men undertook to stop it, but could not, still a third took hold, but stop it they could not. Some of the party said, "Let's test this," so they put a Bible in the cradle and it stopped instantly. They said that was a fair test.

The gun balls would come in through the windows and we would take them and throw them into the river, which is about thirty-six feet deep, and in a few minutes they would come back through the windows, so we were satisfied that the Evil One was at the helm. I saw the house take fire upstairs in ten different places at once. There were plenty to watch the fires, as people came from all parts of the United States and Canada to see for themselves. No less than from twenty to fifty men were there all the time. The bedsteads would move from one side of the room to the other, and the chairs would move when someone was sitting on them and they could not get off. They thought the Devil was going to take them, chair and all. I saw the pot, full of boiling water, come off the fireplace and sail about the room over our heads and never spill a drop, and then return to its starting place. I saw a large black dog sitting on the milk house while it was burning, and thinking it would burn we threw sticks at it, but it would not stir, but, all at once, it disappeared. I saw the mush pot chase the dog that happened to come with one of the neighbours, through a crowd, and the people thought the Devil was in the pot. It chased the dog all over the house and out of doors, and mush stick would strike it first on one side and then on the other. The dog showed fight, and turning round caught hold of the ring in the stick, which swinging, would strike him first on one side of the face and then on the other. It finally let go of the dog's teeth and went back to the pot. I was acquainted with Mr. McDonald and knew him to be an upright man and in good standing in the Baptist Church.

This is my true statement of what I saw.

William S. Fleury

Old McAfee

One of the oldest burial grounds in the Fort Erie area is the McAfee Cemetery. It is the resting place of many United Empire Loyalists.

Local tradition tells of a chapel that stood here but burned to the ground. This happened more than a century ago. Since then there have been reports of phosphorescent lights or "fire-balls" that float and bounce over the ground. Are they "fire-balls" at all? One farmer riding his steed past the cemetery at night spotted the bright ball of light playing among the headstones and realized it to be a lantern that was held aloft by a grisly spectre of a man. The spectre turned on him and pursued him for a distance of more than half a mile. It was only the speed of his steed that saved him from being caught in the spectre's clutches.

Historians remind us that the cemetery bears the name of Samuel McAfee, a local farmer who assisted the rebel William Lyon Mackenzie escape to the United States in the aftermath of the Rebellion of 1837. McAfee disguised Mackenzie as an old woman, passed him off as a member of his family, and rowed the "little rebel" across the Niagara River to Buffalo.

Does McAfee's ghost make his rounds in the cemetery that bears his name, with his bright, bobbing lantern, watching for the return of William Lyon Mackenzie?

The Eldon House Ghost

Eldon House is one of the oldest and most elegant homes in London, Ontario. The gracious mansion, erected in 1834 by the merchant John Harris, served the needs of the Harris family for many generations. It was donated to the city as a museum in 1960 and it has been restored to its high Victorian splendour, with hard-carved furniture, oriental chain, brocaded wallpaper, and safari souvenirs. It is not difficult to imagine the festival balls and formal receptions held in the formal ballroom and dining-room by John Harris and his seven daughters.

One evening in 1856, the following disturbing incident occurred at a formal reception. One of the Harris daughters, Sarah, was engaged to be married. Her fiancé, Lieutenant Wenman Wynniatt, an officer in the British Army then garrisoned in London, was invited to the reception, but the gentleman was uncharacteristically late in arriving. As an officer he was punctual. Sarah kept glancing nervously at the entrance hall, fearing something was amiss. Finally, at 6:00 p.m., the gentleman appeared. He looked remote and distraught. He was dishevelled, and his clothes were muddy. Sarah greeted him and so did her father and one of her sisters. But there was no reply. The gentleman turned away, and without leaving the hallway, disappeared into the night.

They had seen an apparition. The gentleman never did attend the reception. Later that night his riderless horse appeared at the gate of Eldon House. The next day the Army instituted a manhunt and his body was found in a ford of the Thames River. He was presumably riding to Eldon House when he had been thrown by his horse and killed in the fall. His watch had stopped at 6:00 p.m.

Sarah's grief was genuine but brief. She eventually married the Hon. Robert Dalzell. Their marriage was a happy one, and two of their daughters married earls. One wonders, however, whether she ever really came to terms with the apparition of her fiancé.

Welsh Lullabies

The Bishop Fuller House once stood in its glory at the intersection of Thorold Stone Road and Cemetery Road, Thorold, Ontario. It was erected about 1845, and in its day it was a singularly gracious mansion, constructed of stone, with a fan window above the main entrance. It had twenty-one rooms and it had been built to the specifications of Bishop Thomas Brock Fuller to serve as the first rectory of the Anglican Church in Thorold. The ballroom on the second floor was a splendid scene the evening in 1860 when H.R.H. the Prince of Wales, later Edward VII, danced with invited guests into the wee hours of the morning.

Alas, the house has since fallen into wrack and ruin, but what a haunted ruin it is! The site is repeatedly vandalized. Many are the stories told about Bishop Fuller House. Across its halls and down its corridors is said to walk the ghost of a young woman. She is clad in a trailing nightgown that dates from the period of the pioneer settlers. She appears on the second floor and glides from bedroom to bedroom, but vanishes if approached, leaving behind the scent of lavender.

Sometimes the nameless young woman is seen; sometimes, instead, what is seen is the flickering flame of a lighted candle that travels through the air, going from room to room, unsupported by a human hand. The feeling is that a young woman is searching for something or watching over someone.

At dusk there are reports that the sad strains of Welsh lullabies may be heard throughout the second floor, as if being sung by a young woman.

Tom Thomson's Ghost

It is said that on certain mornings, through the mist that rises from Canoe Lake in Algonquin Park, one may discern the spectral form of a youthful outdoorsman who is forlornly but silently paddling his grey canoe across the nervous waters of the mournful lake.

The phantom canoeist is Tom Thomson, the famous painter of the wilds of the north country and the inspiration for the Group of Seven, which was formed some years following his death. Thomson was also an expert woodsman, a master canoeist, and a great outdoorsman. He was in his fortieth year, in perfect health, and he inexplicably drowned. His death — and its aftermath — remain one of Canada's great mysteries.

Thomson was a guest in Mowat Lodge on the west shore of Canoe Lake. On the morning of July 8, 1917, he informed two park guides, who knew him well, that he was leaving to go trout fishing on nearby Gill Lake. Off he went, paddling his favourite grey canoe across Canoe

Lake. Eight days later his body was recovered from the waters of the lake. There was a gash on his right forehead, and his fishing line was found wrapped sixteen or seventeen times around his left ankle. No water was found in his lungs. His canoe was never recovered.

Rumours circulated that Thomson's death was not the result of accident but of foul play. At the time of his death, it was said, he was romantically involved with Winifred Trainor, the beautiful wife of a German-American summer resident of the area. Thomson had argued with her husband about the war then being waged against Germany. They had exchanged words about Winifred. Was he murdered by the German-American?

The mystery of Thomson's death was matched by the mystery of his burial place. Before the arrival of the family's instructions concerning the disposition of the body, the remains were placed in a casket and buried at the tiny hilltop cemetery at Canoe Lake. The following night the casket was disinterred by a stranger, who worked alone by lantern-light through the night. Only later was it learned that the stranger was an undertaker from nearby Huntsville named Churchill, who was acting on instructions from the Thomson family. Churchill had the coffin conveyed to the family home at Leith, near Owen Sound. Once there, it was opened in the presence of family members, the identity of the body was established, and the coffin was reburied at the United Church Cemetery at Leith, where it rests to this day.

Since that fatal day in 1917, numerous guides, fishermen, campers, and tourists have described the misty shapes they have seen moving across the waters of Canoe Lake. They report the progress of a lone, lean paddler in a grey canoe. Occasionally they see the canoe being beached near Hayhurst Point, but when they approach the point to look for the canoe, not only can it not be found but also there are no signs of any human activity in the vicinity.

The most moving words about Tom Thomson appear on the Thomson Cairn at Canoe Lake, which was erected by his friends on September 27, 1917. They were composed by fellow artist J.E.H. MacDonald, and include the following fine tribute: "He lived humbly but passionately with the wild. It made him brother to all untamed things of nature. It drew him apart and revealed itself wonderfully to him. It sent him out from the woods only to show these revelations through his art. And it took him to itself at last."

The ghost of Tom Thomson, as well as his paintings, may be numbered among the "untamed things of nature."

The Vision of Old Walt

Old Walt is the nickname of an immense ridge of Precambrian rock in Ontario's Bon Echo Provincial Park. Old Walt acquired its name in 1919 when the rock was dedicated to the "democratic ideals" of the great American poet Walt Whitman. It was dedicated by a stalwart band of Canadian Whitmanites who were led by Flora Macdonald Denison, pioneer feminist and mother of the writer Merrill Denison.

Horace L. Traubel (1858-1919) was among the guests who were assembled for the dedication ceremony at Bon Echo on August 23, 1919. This was only appropriate; Traubel had been the poet's close friend and was his devoted biographer. Traubel had kept vigil at Whitman's bedside and was present when the poet expired in 1892 at Camden, N.J. Whitman placed a premium on friendship, and Traubel was loyal to the point of death.

Traubel reported experiencing a series of visions of Whitman at Bon Echo before his own death there on September 6, 1919. The third and final vision occurred on his deathbed, two days before he succumbed, and it was witnessed not only by Traubel but also by Lieutenant-Colonel L. Moore Cosgrave, one of the Canadian Whitmanites. As Cosgrave later explained, he and Traubel saw "the likeness of Walt Whitman, standing upright beside the bed...."

Cosgrave's statement took the form of a letter written from his residence in Toronto in late May 1920. It was addressed to Walter Franklin Prince, the psychologist and psychical researcher, and Prince reproduced the statement in his book *Noted Witnesses for Psychic Occurrences* (1928). Thus the statement of Whitman's "likeness" rests not only on Cosgrave's statement but also, as Prince shows, on corroborative evidence from Flora Macdonald Denison and others who were present at Bon Echo that fateful summer.

* * *

With reference to your communication of May 25, in connection with the psychical occurrences connected with the passing of Horace Traubel I hereby state as follows:

During the months of August and September, 1919, I was in close touch with Mr. Horace Traubel, well known for his numerous writings and spiritual plane of thought. Previous to that time I had not known him personally, nor had I a deep knowledge of the works and ideals of Whitman. This I state to show that my mind, conscious or subconscious, had not been engrossed in their works or belief. In addition, my long service in France with the Canadian forces, practically continually in the advanced lines from January, 1915, to the Armistice, had, naturally, made me familiar with the presence of death and the atmosphere around the dying. Though imbuing me with natural reverence, [this] created no unusual tension or emotional excitement such as is common to those unfamiliar with death. This is also stated to indicate that I was in a normal condition when the occurrence took place, to which Mrs. Denison alludes, and I beg to corroborate *in toto* the statements made by her in reference to myself. Briefly, it was as follows: During the three nights previous to the passing of Horace Traubel, I had remained at his bedside, throughout the latter hours of darkness, momentarily expecting the end. My thoughts at all times were very clear and spiritual, owing to the quietude of the surroundings, the close touch of nature and the peculiar clean magnetism that seemed to surround this remarkable selfless man, who had given his whole life to the service of humanity. I had felt this curious spirituality surrounding but few great people, and never with ordinary beings.

During this long watch, Horace Traubel, who was suffering from paralysis and debility, was without visible pain, and semi-conscious, unable to articulate owing to paralysis of the tongue. His eyes, however, which were remarkably brilliant and expressive, gave us the clue to the majority of his needs. On the last night, about 3 a.m., he grew perceptibly weaker, breathing almost without visible movement, eyes closed and seemingly comatose. He stirred restlessly after a long period, and his eyes opened, staring towards the further side of the bed. His lips moved, endeavoring to speak. I moved his head back, thinking he needed more air, but again it moved away, and his eyes remained riveted on a point some three feet above the bed. My eyes were at last drawn irresistibly to the same point in the darkness, as there was but a small shaded night lamp behind a curtain on the further side of the room. Slowly the point at which we were both looking grew gradually brighter. A light haze appeared, spread until it assumed bodily form, and took the likeness of Walt Whitman, standing upright beside the bed, a rough tweed jacket on, an old felt hat upon his head and his right hand in his pocket, similar to a number of his portraits. He was gazing down at Traubel, a kindly, reassuring smile upon his face. He nodded twice as though reassuringly, the features quite distinct for at least a full minute, then gradually faded from sight. My eyes turned back to Traubel, who remained staring for almost another minute, when he also turned away, his features remarkably clear of the strained expression they had worn all evening, and he did not move again until his death, two hours later. I reported the occurrence to Mrs. Denison, who entered the facts in her diary at once, as she had records of several other psychic phenomena to date. I am thoroughly convinced of the exactness of the above statements, and did not regard it as extraordinary, owing to the fact that I had experienced similar phenomena at crucial movements during heavy casualties in France.

Ambrose Small, Missing Man

Charles Fort, the collector of oddities, once noted that Ambrose Small disappeared in Toronto and that Ambrose Bierce disappeared in Mexico, so he came to the conclusion that "somebody is collecting Ambroses"!

Everyone knows that Ambrose Bierce was an American writer who disappeared in revolutionary Mexico in 1914. But not everyone knows that Ambrose Small, Canada's most famous "missing man," disappeared in downtown Toronto in broad daylight. He vanished from history on December 2, 1919, at 5:30 p.m. At the time of his disappearance he was fifty-two years old, the owner of legitimate theatres in seven Ontario cities, and the controller of bookings in sixty-two other houses. He was a self-made millionaire, the equivalent of Edwin Mirvish and Garth Drabinsky all in one.

His absence was noted nationally and internationally. It is worth noting that the day before he disappeared, he concluded the sale of his theatres and deposited $1.7 million in the bank. His wife concluded that he had been done in by a "designing woman." Indeed, the police did discover a "private secret room" off his office in the Grand Opera House near Adelaide and Yonge Streets. For a day or two Sir Arthur Conan Doyle, while visiting New York, showed initial interest in the case. Spirit mediums came up with unlikely scenarios: he was the victim of amnesia, he was embarking on a brand-new life in foreign parts, he was abducted by his private secretary, he was murdered by gamblers or gangsters, he was interred in the basement of the Opera House, he was a prisoner in a lime-kiln near Brampton, Ontario, etc. Harry Blackstone, the famous magician, claimed he recognized Small playing roulette in a gambling casino in Juarez, Mexico. Whatever his fate, Toronto police formally closed the unsolved case of the disappearance of Ambrose Small in 1960.

"The final curtain may be down on the most bizarre melodrama in Canadian theatrical history — but who can be sure?" wrote journalist Murray Rutherford in 1978. "The ghost of Ambrose Small has never rested quietly." How right he was! The ghost of Ambrose Small is said to haunt the old and dignified Grand Theatre on Richmond Street in London, Ontario. This is only right and proper, as it is believed that the Grand in London was the favourite theatre in his entire chain.

The Grand opened its doors in 1901 and Small's spirit took up residence following his disappearance. Theatre folk are a superstitious lot, so it is not surprising that if anything went awry thereafter, during a production or between productions, it was blamed on "Amby," the Ghost of the Grand. Amby had his own box (stage left). Bela Lugosi performed at the Grand. Beatrice Lillie, the Toronto-born toast of vaudeville, appearing in a revue, claimed that a memory lapse saved her life when an arc light fell and shattered centre stage where she should have been standing. Throughout the 1950s and 1960s, actors and stagehands reported seeing Small's ghost walking the wings or standing in the fly-loft. Actors and actresses attributed little mishaps (like clasps on costume jewellery becoming undone) to the spirit of Ambrose, who loved practical jokes. Yet in 1975, when a producer of television documentaries arranged for seven psychics to meet in a circle on the darkened stage of the Grand, not one of the psychics was able to contact the missing man's spirit, although one of the psychics claimed that he had received a spirit-message that said that Ambrose would not be forthcoming. (This has proved to be true, so far!) Still, Small's spirit may well have saved the building from extensive damage. During renovation and restoration work in 1977, a bulldozer clearing debris kept stalling. Good thing it did: it was within inches of knocking down the building's retaining wall. The Grand Theatre is now completely and safely restored to its former Edwardian glory, perhaps thanks to "Amby, the Ghost of the Grand"!

An Early Morning Visitor

Here is a creepy tale. The experience recalls an event that occurred almost fifty years earlier. It originally appeared as "An Early Morning Visitor to the Abandoned Hotel" on a page reserved for true-life ghost stories published in the *Edmonton Journal*, October 30, 1988. The writer is F.D. Blackley, professor emeritus of history, University of Alberta, Edmonton. The narrative recalls a scary episode in the life of the author while still a student in southern Ontario in 1939. It conveys some of the enthusiasm of youth!

In the summer before the outbreak of the Second World War, my girlfriend had a summer job in a small town on Lake Ontario.

One afternoon I hitchhiked from Toronto to see her. We had a pleasant evening, including a walk along the beach. I noticed an abandoned building, presumably an old hotel, a little distance from the water, in a grove of trees. Eventually, I parted with the young lady and had to decide what I should do for the night, as it was now dark.

A university student, I had very little money. I considered the town hotel but it was very close to the chiming town clock, which I knew would bother me. I recalled the abandoned building and thought that I might find a dry spot there on which to curl up until morning.

I went back to the beach and had no problem entering the building. I went to the second floor. This had a long, central hall with many rooms opening from it on either side. I took a room at the far end of the hall with a window that overlooked the roof of a porch. I lay down on a raincoat that I had brought with me.

About 4:00 a.m., while it was still dark, I awakened with a jump. It was as if I had been startled by a loud noise, although I am convinced that this had not been so. I stood up and looked down the hall, lit by a bit of moonlight from a window over the stair. Coming towards me was an indistinct figure with a softly burning lantern.

It was entering each room in turn as if it was looking for someone, or something. As it neared my end of the hall, I saw its face, a horrible one that seemed to drip evil. Worse, perhaps, I could see some of the details of the hall through its body. I did not wait for the lantern-carrier to enter my room. I went out the window onto the porch roof. As I jumped to the ground, I could see the lantern flashing in my "bedroom."

I went uptown and found an all-night truck stop, where I had coffee to calm my nerves, and some breakfast. The cafe wasn't very busy and I was able to ask the proprietor about the abandoned building by the beach. It had been a hotel, he said, but it had not been successful. Some locals, he added, said that it was haunted by an old man with a lantern! He didn't believe the story. I did not tell him that I did.

The Ghost of St. Columbkill's

The Irish abbot and missionary named Columba or Colmcille is recalled in the name of St. Columbkill's Roman Catholic Church. The church building is said to be haunted by the ghost of Father Henry McPhillips (1862-1897), one of its pastors, whose body lies buried in the adjoining cemetery. It is said that his spirit returns periodically to brood over the fortunes of his flock. It floats across the gallery and plays the organ in the church.

In the 1960s, Father Henry's ghost appeared to a group of cleaning women who were at work in the church building. A journalist described what they reported: "A shadowy figure floated across the gallery and, sitting down at the keyboard, started playing the organ. He played beautifully. Some of the watching girls screamed and fled but others stayed to see the figure vanish mysteriously into the belfry." A cleaning woman noted: "We were all cleaning the church when suddenly this figure floated across the gallery and started playing the organ. It was dressed in a black choir gown and black hat with a white face. Only the eyes were visible."

The position of the present pastor on the subject of the ghost is that it is all hearsay and gossip. Yet the popular tradition persists that St. Columbkill's is haunted by the ghost of Father Henry.

The Vision of the Chapel

If any site in Canada is haunted, surely it is Kingsmere. This is the name of the country estate of the late Prime Minister W.L. Mackenzie King. He died here on July 22, 1950, having bequeathed the five-hundred-acre estate to the nation. It is part of Gatineau Park, which every year attracts tens of thousands of tourists and visitors.

In 1934, Mackenzie King began to collect architectural remnants from various structures and sites, including the British Parliament Buildings, and to combine them into his "ruins." Among the picturesque ruins are the Abbey, the Temple, the Cloisters, and the Chapel. At his home Moorside and his cottage Shady Hill, he conducted seances and contacted "the spirits of the departed." Many visitors find the ruins "eerie."

One visitor who found them more than eerie was Gwendolyn MacEwen, who in her poetry and fiction explored the interface between real and imaginary worlds. She first heard about the "ruins" in the early 1960s when she visited Ottawa to recite her poetry. When the evening reading was over, one of her hosts, a practical-minded person and not a poet at all, suggested she might enjoy a late-night ride to Kingsmere to see the ruins. "I had no preconceived notion about the ruins. In fact, I had never even heard of them. But my imagination can do anything!"

By the time they reached Gatineau Park it was close to midnight. They parked the car and began walking towards the ruins when a thunderstorm suddenly struck. Light rain began to fall, and in the distance the ruins were momentarily lit by a flash of lightening. They quickened their pace in order to reach their destination before the rain began to pelt down. Then lightening struck again, brilliantly illuminating the ruins right in front of them. They froze dead in their tracks. They felt very cold. Time stood still. There was a figure standing within the arch of the Chapel, illuminating the night. "Did you see that?" the host asked MacEwen. "I don't want to talk about it," the poet replied. It was eerie. By this time they had turned around and were racing through the pelting rain to the car. They drove back to Ottawa in silence. Even recalling the experience, almost a quarter-century later in August 1987, months before her death, the poet felt fright. "There was something about the figure. It still chills my blood!"

Mackenzie King's Ghost

Everyone knows by now that William Lyon Mackenzie King, Canada's longest-serving prime minister, had an abounding curiosity about the nature of the afterlife. He was a spiritualist. What is less well known is the fact that the late prime minister of Canada, who died at his estate Kingsmere on July 22, 1950, addressed a friend and confidant four years later!

That friend was Percy J. Philip, Scots-born newspaperman and Ottawa-based correspondent for the *New York Times*.

This information became public knowledge on CBC Radio, September 24, 1954. Here is Philip's account of his conversation with the late prime minister. He called it "I Talked with Mackenzie King's Ghost."

⋯◄◖○◗►⋯

On a June evening in 1954 I had a long conversation with the former Canadian Prime Minister William L. Mackenzie King as we sat on a bench in the grounds of his old summer home at Kingsmere, 12 miles from Ottawa. It seemed to me an entirely normal thing although I knew perfectly well that Mr. King had been dead for four years.

Of course, when I returned to Ottawa and told my story nobody quite believed me. I myself became just the least bit uncertain as to whether it really had happened, or at least as to how it had happened. Did I fall asleep and dream? Was this due to paranormal circumstances which cannot be explained?

Of one thing I am sure. Mr. King himself would believe me. He once held similar conversations — almost daily in some cases — with persons who had left this world. He talked with his father and mother regularly and with great men and women of the past. His diary, in which he recorded his spiritual experiences, as well as his political activities and contacts, gives detailed accounts of these conversations. Unfortunately it is not likely to be published in full because his will provided that certain parts should be destroyed. His literary executors feel bound to carry out these instructions.

It was not until after his death that the Canadian people learned that their bachelor, Liberal Prime Minister communed with the dead both directly and, occasionally, through mediums. When it did become known — in a rather sensational way — it shocked many.

Yet the Prime Minister made no secret of his beliefs and practices. To friends who had lost dear ones he wrote in this manner: "I know how you feel. It seems as though you cannot bear to go on without that wonderful companionship and affection. But let me assure you that love still exists. A bond as strong as that is not broken by death or anything else. Your father is still near you. If you can be still and listen and feel, you will realize he is close to you all your life. I know that because it is so with my mother and me."

That quotation is from one of the many hundreds of letters of condolence which Mr. King wrote with his own hand, for he was punctilious in such matters. At funerals he always spoke similar words of comfort to those bereaved. Otherwise, although he made no secret of his beliefs, he did not parade them.

Once, at Government House, about Christmas time in 1945, he told the Governor General, the Earl of Athlone, that he had spoken with President Roosevelt the previous night. "President Truman, you mean," said the Governor. The Earl saw that some of his staff were making signs from behind Mr. King's back, evidently trying to convey some message. He was puzzled but, being a good constitutional Governor General, he kept quiet and did not again correct the Prime Minister when he repeated, "Oh, no, I mean the late President Roosevelt."

The occasion of the incident was the showing of the Noel Coward film, *Blithe Spirit*, which Mr. King found "most interesting."

"It is difficult to imagine the life after death," he said, chatting gaily. "Probably the best thing to do is to regard it as a continuation of the one we know with the same processes of growth and change until, eventually, we forget our life and associations on this earth, just as old people tend to forget their childhood experiences."

His Excellency, who was a brother of the late Queen Mary and a soldier by profession, muttered, "Yes, yes, probably." He obviously was shaken. He had been chosen by Mr. King to be Governor General of Canada and it made him nervous to learn that his Prime Minister was receiving advice from extra-mundane sources.

"Good God," he exclaimed when his staff explained why they had tried to shush him, "is that where the man gets his policies?"

Having an open mind about the occult and being inquisitive by nature, I later managed to turn several conversations with Mr. King to this subject. Once, especially, when we were crossing the Atlantic to Europe, he talked freely about his beliefs and experiences as we walked the deck.

"If one believes in God and a life after death," he said, "it is inevitable that one must believe that the spirits of those who have gone take an interest in the people and places they loved during their lives on earth. It is the matter of communication that is difficult. For myself I have found that the method of solitary, direct, communion is best. After my father and mother died I felt terribly alone. But I also felt that they were near me. Almost accidentally I established contact by talking to them as if they were present and soon I began to get replies."

These and other things that the Prime Minister said to me at different times came back to my mind as, on that June evening, I drove up the Kingsmere road and was reminded by a sign that the estate of Moorside, which Mr. King had left to the Canadian people in his will, lay just ahead.

It is a beautiful place. There are 550 acres of woodland and clearings, through most of which everyone is free to wander at will. A little stream with a waterfall flows through it down to the valley below. Mr. King accumulated it almost acre by acre, adding steadily in his methodical way to the original lot he had bought when he first came to Ottawa at the beginning of the century. His quick temper seldom flashed more hotly than when he discovered that some neighbor had sold a parcel of land without giving him a chance to buy. Adding to his estate became a passion with the future Prime Minister. There he loved to receive visitors and also to be alone.

In buying the land Mr. King showed his Scottish shrewdness. But the building of the "ruins" was a perfect example of that romantic daftness that sometimes bewitches the supposedly hard-headed Scot. The direction sign now set up for tourists calls them "ruins" but the uninformed must wonder what they once were. There were doorways and windows, a fireplace, a row of columns, which Mr. King called the cloisters, coats of arms carved in stone, bits and pieces of the old Parliament Buildings, the mint, banks and private houses all built into an artistic enough and wholly whimsical suggestion of a ruined castle. Somehow, perhaps because the surroundings with outcrop rock and pine are so fitting, they escape being silly.

On that evening there were no other visitors. The air was clear and cool. I sat down on a bench beside the ruins and thought about the strange little man who loved his hill-top home so dearly. I suppose I was in what I called a receptive mood. Although I had not then read it I was following the instructions in that letter from which I already have quoted, to "be still and listen and feel."

I became conscious that I was not alone. Someone sat on the park bench beside me.

There were no sighs, groans and lightning flashes such as mark a spirit's arrival on the Shakespearean stage. There was, if anything, a deeper peace. Through a fold in the hills I could see a stretch of the broad Ottawa Valley. I tried to concentrate on it and keep contact with the normal but the presence on the bench would not be denied.

Without turning my head, for somehow I feared to look, I said as naturally as I could, "Good evening, Mr. King."

In that warm tone which always marked his conversation the voice of Mr. King replied, "Good evening, Philip. I am so glad you spoke to me."

That surprised me. "I was thinking of you," I muttered.

"Oh, yes," he replied. "I knew that. But one of the rules which govern our conduct on this side is that we are like the children and must not speak unless we are spoken to. I suppose it is a good rule because it would be very disturbing if we went around talking to people. The sad thing is that so few of them ever talk to us."

Here I think I should say that the reader must decide for himself whether or not he believes this story. It puzzles me greatly.

"I suppose," I said, or I think I said, resuming the conversation, "that we are just a bit scared. You know how hard it is to speak into a dark, empty room."

"That certainly is a difficulty for many people," Mr. King said. "But the room is never really empty. It is often filled with lonely ones who would like to be spoken to. They must, however, be called by name, confidently, affectionately, not challenged to declare themselves."

"Your name," I said, "must often be so mentioned in this lovely place you bequeathed to the Canadian people."

"Oh, yes, mentioned," he said. I glanced at him and seemed to see his eyes sparkle as they did in life, for he had a great deal of puckish humor. "But between being mentioned and being addressed by name, as you addressed me, there is a great deal of difference. I have heard things about my character, motives, political actions and even my personal appearance and habits that have made me laugh so loudly I thought I must break the sound barrier. And I have heard things about myself, too, that have made me shrink."

In the evening silence I had the sensation of being suspended in time and space as the quiet voice went on. "There are things that I said and did that I could regret but, on this side, we soon learn to have no regrets. Life would be meaningless if we did not all make mistakes, and eternity intolerable if we spent it regretting them."

He paused and I thought he looked at me quizzically. "By the way," he said, "do you still write for the *New York Times*?"

When I said that I had retired he chuckled. "But still," he said, "I think I had better not give indiscreet answers to your questions."

I asked several but he answered with the same skill as marked his replies to questions in the House of Commons and at meetings with the press, divulging nothing. It was I who was the interviewed. He was eager for news and it surprised me then, as it does now, that he seemed not to know fully what was happening in the world. The dead, I discovered, are not omniscient. Or perhaps what we think important is not important to them.

We talked of the development of Canada, of housing and new enterprises like the St. Lawrence Seaway. "My successor has been lucky," Mr. King said. That was as far as he went in any personal reference. "Canada has been very prosperous. I hope it will continue to be so. But you cannot expect good times always. It is adversity that proves the real value of men and nations."

The conversation drifted to the international scene, to philosophic discussion of forms of government, of the balance between Liberty and Authority, the growth and decay of nations and of systems. I cannot tell how long it lasted but I noticed that the sickle moon was getting brighter. I mentioned the time, fumbling for my watch.

"Time," said Mr. King, "I had almost forgotten about time. I suppose I spend a great deal of time up here. There is so much beauty and peace. I gave it to the Canadian people but in a way I have preserved it for myself. It is good to have some familiar, well-loved place to spend 'time' in, until one gets used to eternity."

We both rose from the bench — or at least I did. When I looked at him, as I then did for the first time directly, he seemed just as I had known him in life, just as when I had talked with him once at this very spot.

"I think you told me once that you are Scottish born and a wee bit 'fey'," he said. "It's a good thing to be. We have two worlds. Those people who think their world is the only one, and who take it and themselves too seriously, have a very dull time. Do come back and talk with me again."

I muttered words of thanks and then, following the habit of a lifetime, stretched out my hand to bid goodbye. He was not there.

In January 1955 Philip published a follow-up article in *Liberty* magazine, entitled "My Conversation with Mackenzie King's Ghost."

So many people have asked me to tell them "the real truth" about my recent "interview" with the late Prime Minister Mackenzie King on the park bench at Kingsmere, Que., that I am glad to have the opportunity offered me by *Liberty*, to fill in the background and correct some misunderstandings, of the "ghost story" which I told over the CBC network last September 24.

Perhaps I should begin by saying that in Scotland, where I was born, we believe in ghosts. My father, who was a minister of the Church of Scotland, told me how his father had come to him in dreams, and on the edge of sleep, so vividly he could not afterwards believe that it was not real. Even more oddly, though he died at the age of 86 when I was three years old, my gaunt old grandfather, wrapped in his homespun plaid, has paid me several visits. Afterwards, I could not say definitely whether I had been asleep or awake. But the whole conversation, even to the old man's slight Aberdeenshire accent, was so vivid that I was positive it had actually taken place.

And that is how it was in my conversation with Mr. King on the park bench among the ruins at Kingsmere last June.

What the explanation may be of such phenomena I do not claim to understand. They may be due to psychic influence, to a stimulated imagination, or to that subconscious working of the mind which happens in dreams.

Yet there is no incompatibility between being a Christian and church-goer, as Mr. King was, and being a searcher into the mystery of the hereafter. During his life, we had several discussions on the fascinating subject, and it came to me as a surprise when, after his death, it was "revealed" in a magazine article that he had been a practising spiritualist. I thought everybody knew about it.

Like many others of his friends, I resented this, perhaps unintentional, exposure of Mr. King to ridicule. Perhaps I should have been warned not to touch such a sensitive subject. There may be no witches in Canada, but there are witch-hunters.

Still I have been a reporter all my life, and I could not resist trying to write an account of that strange experience at Kingsmere. I did it with the greatest care.

I offered what I had written to a national Canadian magazine — not *Liberty* — but it was courteously rejected. I was told later it had gone to the fiction department and had not been regarded as very good fiction.

So I redrafted it for broadcasting. I thought that my Scottish voice might convey my meaning with more subtlety than the cold printed word. I stress its unusual character, I called the talk *Fantasio*. As I would have a much wider audience on the air, I strengthened the warnings that it should not be taken too literally, writing that I was not sure that I believed my story myself, and prefacing my account of the "facts" with the conditional phrase — "If in the mystery of life and the hereafter, there are such things as facts."

That, it seemed to me, provided the key to the story. It was a mystery, and a pleasant one.

The CBC editors, to whom the script was submitted, read it understandingly, and accepted it for broadcasting.

Listeners from one end of the country to another seem also to have understood. Two of Mr. King's literary executors, who have had access to all his private papers, and a former member of his cabinet, were enthusiastic about the portrait I had drawn of their old leader.

But when we come to the treatment of the story by the press, that is another matter.

It perhaps ill becomes one who has been a newspaper reporter all his life, and has undoubtedly made his full measure of mistakes of interpretation and even of fact, to be critical of his colleagues who may fall into error.

I find, however, that some account of how my broadcast was handled by the press is necessary for the proper understanding of the Legend of the Bench at Kingsmere.

That legend has already travelled far beyond Canada. It has brought more than 200 letters, from every province and from many states of the American union. Every weekend, and even during the week, hundreds of visitors have been flocking up to Moorside and arguing hotly whether or not the "ghost" really appeared. The delegates of the Colombo Plan conference in Ottawa have carried the story to the ends of the earth. Political commentators have seized on it as a peg on which to hang pontifical articles. Collins, in the Montreal *Gazette*, lifted it to a high point of humor with his cartoon of Prime Minister St. Laurent sitting on the bench among the ruins, looking pensively upward and asking: "Have you anything to say to *me*?"

But the condensed version of the talk circulated by the Canadian Press was not so well inspired. Probably it was the first time that that news agency had ever put a ghost story on its wires. Certainly it was the first time a CP staff member, in the Ottawa bureau, had ever been asked to provide one.

It was no excuse that the poor fellow had not heard the broadcast. The first thing to do, of course, was to secure the text. There was none available at the CBC studios, as the broadcast had been recorded. I live at Aylmer, Ont., 10 miles from Ottawa, and apparently the CP Ottawa bureau is not equipped to send an intelligent reporter so far to get a story.

I soon found it was impossible to get the facts, nuances, qualifications, suggestions, anecdotes and imponderables into position by telephone. After a struggle, I consented to drive in myself with the text. I might, I thought, be able to keep the story from running wild.

My efforts were wasted. The CP had asked for a ghost story, and the more I insisted that the subject was delicate and the treatment whimsical, the more certain I became that the ghost story I had told over the CBC network, and the one that would be printed, would have little resemblance.

What a fool I had been. I had thought that my broadcast might stir some interest, but I had definitely under-estimated its impact on the ghost-hungry newspaper mind. It made the front pages all across Canada, pushing aside the argument then in progress between Mr. St. Laurent and Quebec Premier Maurice Duplessis.

There were odd little changes. Whereas I had said Mr. King talked to me, the headlines ran that I had talked with Mr. King. The title word, *Fantasio*, became "Fantastic," which is quite different. Sentences were transposed and others, which had seemed so important to me, were entirely omitted.

Not a single newspaper published the text of the talk. Even those, to which a copy had been sent in advance, preferred to publish the CBC version, rather than go to the trouble of writing their own.

The telephone began ringing. Was it true? Argument was warm.

Editors began telegraphing their Ottawa correspondents: Had Philip gone "crackers"? One wit, of sorts, telephoned to ask what brand of whisky I drank.

At 8:30 a.m., on the following Sunday, one of the most enterprising and joyous of my colleagues burst into my cottage, shouting gaily: "The question is — is it true, or is it not true?"

There were others who did not bother even to telephone but began writing freely, interviewing parsons, chauffeurs, CBC officials and residents of Kingsmere.

In the press, the skeptics certainly outnumbered the believers, but the latter were much more industrious in writing private letters. Two spiritualists told of recent conversations with Mr. King who, they said, had confirmed my story. I shall not call them witnesses.

The Haunting of Mackenzie House

Mackenzie House is one of the most historic homes in Toronto. Since 1960 the Toronto Historical Board has maintained it as a museum. Despite the fact that Mackenzie House has been called the most haunted house in Toronto — and perhaps the most haunted house in all of Canada — it is the policy of the Board to maintain that Mackenzie House is not haunted. Guides dressed in period costume who escort visitors through its halls and rooms, which are furnished to recall the period of the 1860s, make no mention of reports of ghosts or poltergeists or mysterious happenings.

Today the residence bears the proud name of William Lyon Mackenzie (1795-1861). Mackenzie was the energetic publisher of the *Colonial Advocate*, first mayor of the City of Toronto in 1834, the promoter of responsible government, and the leader of the Rebellion of 1837 in Upper Canada. When the rebellions were suppressed, Mackenzie fled (dressed as a woman) and found refuge in New York State. There he continued his agitation. With the amnesty he returned to Toronto in triumph. He is known to this day as "the firebrand."

The three-storey brick residence at 82 Bond Street, erected in the 1850s, was acquired and presented to him by grateful friends in recognition of public service. He lived in the house from 1859 until his death in the second-floor bedroom on August 28, 1861. Isabel Grace King, his youngest daughter, also lived and died in the residence. She was the wife of the lawyer John King and the mother of William Lyon Mackenzie King.

William Lyon Mackenzie King (1874-1950), the grandson of William Lyon Mackenzie, was born at "Woodside" in Berlin (now Kitchener), Ontario. The grandson took great pride in the grandfather's commitment to responsible government. He studied law and went on to become Canada's tenth prime minister and the country's most curious and long-lasting leader. It is now known that throughout his life Mackenzie King was fascinated with spiritualism and with the question of human survival after death. Indeed, one of his friends, the correspondent Percy J. Philip, claimed that in 1954 the ghost of Mackenzie King joined him and conversed with him for some time on a park bench at Kingsmere, Mackenzie King's country estate in the Gatineau region of Quebec. While Mackenzie King's spiritualistic beliefs and practices are well documented, the views of his grandfather, William Lyon Mackenzie, go unrecorded. Yet it is hard to believe that the grandfather, who was Scottish-born, was unfamiliar with the subject.

There are no reports of any psychical occurrences in Mackenzie House prior to 1956; there are none of substance later than 1966. The earliest accounts come from a responsible couple, Mrs. and Mrs. Charles Edmunds. They were the house's first live-in, caretaking couple. They occupied Mackenzie House from August 13, 1956, to April 1960 and only left because of the disturbances. They were followed by Mr. and Mrs. Alex Dobban, who arrived in April 1960. The Dobbans, complaining of the same disturbances as the Edmundses, left that June. Archdeacon John Frank of Holy Trinity Anglican Church was called to conduct an exorcism in the parlour, which he did in the presence of reporters on July 2, 1960. Since that time the house's caretakers have lived off the premises, but workmen on the premises and visitors have intermittently complained of disturbances.

The most intelligent discussion — and debunking — of the ghostly happenings at Mackenzie House was conducted by Joe Nickell in one chapter of his book *Secrets of the Supernatural: Investigating the World's Occult Mysteries* (Buffalo: Prometheus Books, 1988). Nickell is both a professional stage magician and a licensed private investigator. He has both prosaic and highly imaginative explanations for all the disturbances. Although he writes well, the story he has to tell is not as gripping as the stories that were told by members of the Edmunds family.

Mr. and Mrs. Charles Edmunds, the first caretaking couple, lived in the house for four years. Their reports are included here, as are the shorter reports of their son Robert and his wife Minnie, who were guests in the house. The four reports first appeared in the *Toronto Telegram* on June 28, 1960, as part of a series entitled "The Ghosts that Live in Toronto," written by the paper's enterprising reporter Andrew MacFarlane. The series appeared following the refusal of the Dobbans' to remain in the house. MacFarlane secured sworn affidavits from all four members of the Edmunds family. They are reproduced here in a slightly edited form.

————— ◆◦❁◦◆ —————

Mrs. Charles Edmunds:

From the first day my husband and I went to stay at the Mackenzie

Homestead, we could hear footsteps on the stairs when there was nobody in the house but us.

The first day, when I was alone in the house, I could hear someone clearly, walking up the stairs from the second floor to the top. Nearly every day there were footsteps at times when there was no one there to make them.

One night I woke up at midnight. I couldn't sleep, although I am normally a good sleeper. I saw a Lady standing over my bed. She wasn't at the side, but at the head of the bed, leaning over me. There is no room for anyone to stand where she was. The bed is pushed up against the wall.

She was hanging down, like a shadow, but I could see her clearly. Something seemed to touch me on the shoulder to wake me up. She had long hair hanging down in front of her shoulders, not black or grey or white, but dark brown, I think. She had a long narrow face. Then it was gone.

Two years ago, early in March, I saw the Lady again. It was the same — except this time she reached out and hit me. When I woke up, my left eye was purple and bloodshot.

I also saw the man at night, a little bald man in a frock coat. I would just see him for a few seconds, and then he would vanish.

I often saw one or the other standing in the room — at least eight or nine times.

A year ago last April, I told my husband: "I have to get out of here." I had to get out of that house. If I didn't get out, I knew I'd be carried out in a box.

I think it was the strain all the time that made me feel this way. I went from 130 pounds to 90 pounds. I wasn't frightened, but it was getting my nerves down.

It was just like knowing there was someone watching you from behind all the time, from just over your shoulder.

Sometimes we'd sit watching the television. My husband might look up all of a sudden at the doorway. I knew what it was. You felt that someone had just come in.

My son and his wife heard the piano playing at night when they were staying with us. When my husband and my son went to look — it stopped.

We could feel the homestead shaking with a rumbling noise some nights. It must have been the press in the basement. We thought at first it might be the subway. But we were too far from the subway....

I did not believe in ghosts when I went to stay at the Mackenzie Homestead. But I do now. It's the only explanation I can think of.

I wish to say that I would not say anything against the Mackenzies. They were hard-working people and so are we. They were not hard on us ... it's just that the house was a strain on the nerves.

Mr. Charles Edmunds:

Certain happenings during the three years and eight months my wife and I served as caretakers of the Mackenzie Homestead have convinced me that there is something peculiar about the place.

On one occasion my wife and I were sleeping in the upstairs bedroom. She woke me up in the middle of the night and said that she had seen a man standing beside her bed.

My wife, to my certain knowledge, knew nothing of Mackenzie or his history. All of the pictures in the homestead show Mackenzie as a man with hair on his head. The man my wife saw and described to me was completely bald with side-whiskers. I had read about Mackenzie. And I know that the man she described to me was Mackenzie. He wore a wig to cover his baldness. But she did not know this.

On another occasion, just after we moved in, my two grandchildren Susan (then aged 4) and Ronnie (then aged 3) went from the upstairs bedroom down to the second-floor bathroom at night.

A few minutes later there were terrific screams. I went down and they were both huddled in the bathroom, terrified. They said there was a Lady in the bathroom. I asked where she was now and they said she just disappeared.

On another night my wife woke up screaming. She said: "There was a small man standing over my bed." She described Mackenzie.

Another night, a woman came up to the bed and looked at my missus. She was a little woman, about my wife's height. My wife said: "Dad — there was a woman here." I told her she was dreaming.

Another night my wife woke up and woke me. She was upset. She said the Lady had hit her. There were three red welts on the left side of her face. They were like finger marks. The next day her eye was bloodshot. Then it turned black and blue. Something hit her. It wasn't me. And I don't think she could have done it herself. And there wasn't anyone else in the house.

On another occasion something peculiar happened with some flowers we had in pots on a window ledge inside the house. This was in winter and we had the geraniums inside. We watered the plants twice a week, on Sundays and Wednesdays.

On a Saturday morning we found that they had all been watered, although we hadn't done it. There was water spilled all over the plants and the saucers they were standing in were full. There was mud on the curtains, and holes in the earth as if someone had poked their fingers in the earth. There was water on the dressing table. Neither of us had watered the plants, and neither had anyone else.

We often heard footsteps on the stairs. Thumping footsteps like someone with heavy boots on. This happened frequently when there was no one in the house but us, when we were sitting together upstairs.

The whole house used to shake with a rumbling sound sometimes. My wife is convinced that this was Mackenzie's press.

I am not an imaginative man, and I do not believe in ghosts. But the fact is that the house was strange enough so that we had to leave.

We would have stayed if it had not been for these happenings. But my wife could not stand it any longer.

Robert Edmunds:

One night my wife woke me up. She said she heard the piano playing downstairs. I heard it, too. I can not remember what the music was like, but it was the piano downstairs playing.

Dad and I went downstairs. When we got to the last landing before the bottom the piano stopped.

It was similar with the printing press in the basement. My wife heard it first and wakened me. I heard it, too. I identified the sound because it was the same as old presses I'd seen in movies and on television. A rumbling, clanking noise — not like modern presses. When Dad and I went downstairs to see about it, it stopped when we reached the same landing.

We heard the piano three or four times, the press just once.

I was not walking in my sleep. I heard them. I don't know what the explanation is. I am not prepared to say I saw any ghosts or apparitions. But I can say that I dreamt more in that house than I ever have before or since.

I do not believe in ghosts. But I find it hard to explain what we heard.

Mrs. Minnie Edmunds.

When my husband and I were staying at Mackenzie Homestead I heard the piano playing downstairs at night three or four times.

We discovered that there was no one downstairs to play it these times, and yet I heard it distinctly. Each time, I woke my husband, and when he and his father went downstairs to investigate it, it stopped.

On one other occasion I heard the printing press running in the basement. I woke my husband, and he and his father went to investigate it. It stopped.

It is not possible to operate the press, because it is locked, and on the occasions when I heard the piano, there was no one downstairs to play it. I can find no natural explanation for these occurrences.

The Haunted Bookshop

Bookshops are haunted by book lovers. One shop that was said to be haunted by "an authenticated apparition" was the Country Bookshop in Lloydtown, a community south of Schomberg, which in turn lies north of Metropolitan Toronto.

The Country Bookshop was opened in a remodelled barn in 1967 by Art Gray, a bibliophile whose specialty was Canadian history and pioneer life. He ran the shop until his death in 1984. Then his widow Audrey ran it for a couple of years more. When it closed, there were over 15,000 volumes on its shelves.

Art Gray was proud of the bookshop's ghost. "Our ghost is an authenticated apparition," he told a reporter. "She is a solid-looking figure. A lady in a cloak, hooded. You never see her face. She starts at twilight — at the walnut tree at the top of the driveway — and walks slowly, up or down. Many people have seen her. But she doesn't bother anyone. She's quite harmless, part of the family really."

According to local tradition, there was a tragedy on the property in the early days of the 1900s. A young mother lost her little baby. She may have killed it herself, or it may have been taken from her. Whichever was the case, the baby was lost to her. The ghost is that of the young mother who even in death seems to be searching, looking about longingly, as if for a lost child. The spirit was anything but malevolent. Apparently dogs wagged their tails when the apparition is felt or seen.

The Country Bookshop is no more. Perhaps the ghost of the young mother still walks the driveway searching for her lost child.

Elizabeth the Ghost

Elizabeth is the ghost that will not leave the historic Hawley-Breckenridge House in Niagara-on-the-Lake. The imposing residence was built in the Southern Colonial style in 1796. The earliest reports of it being haunted were made after 1899, when it was acquired by Major Charles Stanley Herring, an officer with the British Army in India. He reported seeing the ghost of a woman in a long grey dress who "disappeared like smoke" on at least one occasion.

Aileen and Frank Hawley, who knew nothing of its ghostly occupant at the time of purchase, acquired the house in 1953. Soon they grew accustomed to the knocker on the front door sounding and to raps on the back door when no one was there. They and their guests reported seeing the ghostly figure of a young woman on the main floor of the older parts of the building. She appeared to be in her thirties and was wasp-waisted in the fashion of an earlier time. She was wearing a long dress and had on a bonnet that was tied under her chin. She had a gentle face and was called Elizabeth. A psychic who said she saw the spirit said it was the ghost of a woman who had died in the house in the mid-1800s after devoting many years to the care of her parents. It appeared she did not relish leaving the house, preferring to die there than to leave it. Aileen Hawley described Elizabeth's appearance in these words in 1982: "She walks or stands for a few seconds, then disappears; but it's not a frightening experience. It's just as if she's checking to see if everything's okay."

The Haunting of Glanmore

One would have to travel far and wide to find a residence more splendid than Glanmore. With its many notable architectural and artistic features, it recalls the Victorian period in all its bizarre beauty. It is the pride of Belleville, Ontario.

The three-storey house was built in the elaborate Second Empire style complete with mansard roof. The interior is marked by ornate and intricate woodwork and a great many of the house's original furnishings are on display. A magnificent suspended staircase, described as the largest of its kind between Montreal and Toronto, dominates the hall and takes awed visitors from the first to the second floor.

The mansion was erected in 1883 for the Belleville financier John P.C. Phillips, his wife Harriet, and their children, and it has served as the gracious home for three generations of the Phillips and Faulkner families. Eventually the property was donated by the family to the City of Belleville and the County of Hastings to serve as the centrepiece and office of the Hastings County Museum.

Representatives of the Hastings County Museum have no answers to such questions as "Is Glanmore haunted?" or "Was it haunted?" Members of the Phillips and Faulkner families maintain that the house was haunted at least during the period of their residency.

It was Philippa Faulkner who donated Glanmore to the City of Belleville. She was born in the house in 1917. She now lives in Toronto where she is a painter and a long-time member of the Royal Canadian Academy. She recalls that the house had its peculiarities. There was always something odd about the book-lined study on the second floor. From time to time it was pressed into service as an extra bedroom, but her son Sandy and her daughter Anne refused to sleep there, and the maids never wanted to do any of their tasks in that room. To this day it retains a glum air.

Mrs. Faulkner's husband George Faulkner, a prominent physician, died on March 23, 1955. Some nights later Mrs. Faulkner was asleep in the master bedroom. She woke up, felt a presence in the room, looked up, and saw standing at the bedside the figure of a soldier wearing a red coat and a tall white hat. The soldier turned to her, smiled, and vanished. Mrs. Faulkner always felt that the spectre was the spirit of her father's late brother who had fought in the Boer War. She took consolation in the fact that there was someone to watch over her now that she was a widow with young children to raise.

She also recalled the visit that Stephen Leacock, Jr., made to the house about 1941. This was not the famous humorist but his son, a crippled and dwarfish man whom many described as selfish and self-centred. He was in Belleville to visit his sister Daisy Leacock Burrowes, who lived in a house down the street. Leacock, Jr., also visited Glanmore, and when he learned about the ghosts, he led everyone up the stairs to the attic where he found a "cold spot" which he said was the source of the disturbances.

Perhaps there was something in the attic. There was certainly an ill omen. In 1946, the night before the wedding of Philippa and George, there was a crash in the master bedroom. A circle of plaster had dislodged from the ceiling close to the "cold spot" in the attic and had crashed to the floor.

Mrs. Faulkner recalled that the grand piano in the main drawing room played all by itself at night and in the dark. Her heavy bedroom door would slip its lock and creak open by itself. She sensed that the spirit of her grandmother, Harriet (Hattie) Phillips, was walking through the room. Hattie could be seen out of the corner of the eye, and her footfalls could be heard along with the swish of her skirt.

There was always something happening in the house. "Anyone going into that house, if they stood still for a while, would feel something," Mrs. Faulkner noted. These disturbances were more annoying than they were frightening. Nonetheless, in 1963 she summoned a Roman Catholic priest. The young priest donned a white chasuble and went from room to room and walked up and down the stairs, sprinkling holy water and performing the rite of exorcism. Thereafter there were no major disturbances, but there were some minor ones.

Mrs. Faulkner's daughter Anne was born in the house in 1951 and lived there off and on until 1970. One of her pleasures was playing on the grand piano in the main drawing room. One afternoon, engrossed in playing a composition by Debussy, or possibly Rachmaninoff, she suddenly became aware of a presence. She stopped playing, turned around, and watched in startled wonder as a little woman, under five feet in height, with red hair, wearing a grey silk dress, with a set of keys fastened dangling from her waist, crossed the room, and disappeared as suddenly as she had appeared.

Somewhat surprised and frightened, Anne told her mother. Mrs. Faulkner explained that Anne had just seen the ghost of Harriet (Hattie) Phillips, the long-dead wife of the financier who had built the house. The description fit Hattie, and so did the bustle, as Hattie had kept herself busy decorating and painting the house, notably the ceiling of the dining room.

Anne was a nighthawk. At three o'clock in the morning, she would tiptoe down the suspended staircase, make her way to the kitchen, and then tiptoe back up the stairs to her room with a cup of tea. (Today the room displays modern art and is called the Manley MacDonald Room.) On a number of occasions, she felt there was a presence walking up the stairs close behind her. So frightened was she that she would carry the cup close to her shoulder, so she could pitch the hot tea at whomever or whatever it was that was stalking her.

Is Glanmore haunted? Was it haunted? There have been no reports of hauntings in recent years. In fact, there have been none since the building was acquired by the Hastings County Museum. Perhaps the ghost of Hattie and the ghost of the red-coated soldier are lurking in the halls and corridors awaiting a suitable occasion for a sudden appearance and then an equally sudden disappearance.

The Screaming Tunnel

Visitors go to Niagara Falls to see the mighty cataracts, but they seldom inquire about the Screaming Tunnel, despite the fact it was featured in David Cronenberg's horror movie *The Dead Zone*, which was based on the Stephen King novel. There are many stories about the Screaming Tunnel, a genuinely scary place. Here is one of them.... It comes from Fred Habermehl, an area resident who lives in Niagara Falls, who wrote to me about it on April 19, 1996.

———— •=►❮❯❯►◄►•• ————

After one passes over the Skyway on the road to Niagara Falls, the Queen Elizabeth Way climbs the escarpment at a point known locally as Sand Plant Hill. Two hundred metres to the west of the highway, there is an old tunnel under the train tracks, known to the youngsters as "the screaming tunnel." A path leads through the tunnel and up the hill into the fields. The story they tell is of a farmhouse that once stood on top of the hill. It caught fire one night and burned to the ground. A young girl ran screaming down the path with her nightclothes on fire. She burned to death in the tunnel. Ever since, if you light a match in the tunnel, a scream is heard and the match goes out.

A number of years ago, I took a carload of young girls out to investigate this phenomenon. We made our way, with some apprehension, through the mud and into the tunnel. I struck a match. Surely enough, there was a scream and the match went out. None of the girls would admit to screaming. When we walked on up the path, there is a thicket of trees between the field and the highway. We found evidence of a structure that had been destroyed. There was also a great concrete block inscribed on top with the letters, R.I.P.

The Bilotti House

They say a ghost never really goes away. The same thing might be said about a good ghost story.

One Sunday night in June of 1971, Norm Bilotti was startled out of his sleep by the screaming of his wife Sherri, who was lying in bed beside him. He opened his eyes and saw what was frightening her. The two of them could make out the long, black, gowned shape of a faceless spectre, which for a few seconds hovered a few feet above the bed, disappearing before the lights could be turned on. They were shaken and could not explain their experience.

Exactly twenty-eight days later the spectre appeared again in the same way, but this time they could discern more detail. The spectre was a life-sized, legless woman, with bulging eyes and hair standing on end as though she was receiving an electric shock.

The Bilottis reported their experience to the press and the account of their experiences attracted wide interest. A professional psychic named Malcolm Bessent of the Human Dimensions Institute of Rosary Hill College in Buffalo came to examine the two-storey house on Upper Wellington Street in Hamilton. He was accompanied on his rounds by Bernard Baskin, a respected Hamilton rabbi with a special interest in witchcraft, Dr. A.S. MacPherson, former clinical director of the Hamilton Psychiatric Hospital, and John Bryden, reporter for the *Hamilton Spectator*, which covered the case in detail.

In his tour of the house Bessent paused in the bedroom where the disturbances had occurred. He said that he sensed that the problems in the house were connected with the previous occupants, a family of four. He said that a woman had died a painful death in the house. The letters S.A. came to his mind and these could be the first letters in a name, perhaps hers. The sight of green and white flowers presented itself, as did the date August 1947.

According to John Bryden, who reported on the tour of the house, the psychic was correct or close to the truth on some details but misleading or wide of the mark on others. A search of the title of the property revealed that it had been purchased in September 1947. The maiden name of the woman who had lived in the house was Flowers. She had not died in the house, but had suffered a long, painful illness there. When she lapsed into unconsciousness, she was rushed to the local hospital where she died. She was the mother of four children. Someone suggested that the letters S.A. referred to the Salvation Army, as she and her husband were members of that organization.

The psychic did not establish any connection between the previous occupants and the spectre. But he did note that there was something odd about the bedroom area. "There's something about this house that this phenomenon is trying to attract attention to," Bessent claimed. "Maybe something under the floor. Definitely something has happened or is in this house that attention is being drawn to. I think something is concealed in this area — what, I don't know. I'm being drawn to it very strongly. It's the reason for the manifestation." An examination of the house revealed nothing unusual.

The spectre of the haunted house of Upper Wellington Street was a nine-day wonder. No further disturbances were reported for eleven years. But some stories will not die or go away for long.

The Bilottis eventually moved out of the house and it was slated for demolition in October 1982. One member of the wrecking crew claimed that he heard strange sounds as he went about his noisy work. Then, between the walls of the second floor, workmen uncovered the upper half of a large tombstone, a marker meant for a double grave. One half was marked "Our Baby" and inscribed "Martha Louisa" with the date

"1888." The other half was inscribed "Emma Grace" and dated "9 Nov. 1879." Mark McNeil of the *Hamilton Spectator* established that the stones were the memorials of two infants, Martha Louisa Young and Emma Grace Young, who died and were buried in the local cemetery not far away. How their tombstones, which were missing from the cemetery, had ended up between the walls of the building, erected about 1942, was anyone's guess. Why the Bilottis were disturbed in their sleep on two occasions in 1971 is as least as odd and mysterious.

The Beautiful Lady in White

Mrs. M. Kirkpatrick is a resident of North Woodstock, Ontario. She was born in Chelsea, England. She read my request for true-life "ghost stories" in the Woodstock weekly newspaper, the *Sentinel-Review*, and sent me her own account of the appearance of the Beautiful Lady in White in 1965 or 1966. I received the handwritten letter on May 25, 1990.

The account is interesting in two ways. Although the ghost was not seen by Mrs. Kirkpatrick, it was seen by both her young son and her adult house guest. She later learned that there was a local tradition about a wandering spirit that inhabits small stone houses or cottages, as well as the story of a suicide in her own house.

It seems that local lore buttresses local experiences. Or is it the other way round?

―――――――――

I once rented a stone house on a farm at R.R. 7, Woodstock. The house was later burnt down, but its remains are still to be seen.

I lived there with my two boys, then ten years old and twelve years old. They slept in separate bedrooms upstairs. We were in the house several years.

It was getting towards Christmas. One night, my younger son told me the next morning, a beautiful lady in white came into his room and smiled at him. This happened for a few nights in a row.

Once I had some friends stay overnight. I put one of them in my younger son's room. Nobody had mentioned his story about the beautiful lady in white, especially not me, as nobody else had seen this lady.

Anyway, the next morning, our guest came down. He asked me if I had gone into his room. I said no, because I had no reason at all to go upstairs or into his room. Anyway, as he described it, this beautiful woman in white came into the room, looked at him, smiled, and then went away.

By this time I was getting "the willies." I decided to move back into town. I figured the house must be haunted and the ghost must be a beautiful lady.

By this time it was very near Christmas of the following year. I was about to have another child.

One day I picked up the *Sentinel-Review* and read about a ghost. There was this story of "The Lady in White." Evidently she was about to marry and her future husband had built a little stone house for her. He got killed in a crash on the eve of their wedding. So she went around to all the stone houses looking for her husband. She was harmless, according to the article.

I never saw her, but my son, who is now forty-two years old, will swear to this day that he saw the Lady in White. My guest saw her, too, but unfortunately he is now deceased.

I found out afterwards that a man's wife left him and he hanged himself in the little stone house in which we lived.

I believe in ghosts, as I saw two myself in England. I saw the famous ghost of Dr. Phene, well known on King's Road in Chelsea, and I saw the spirit of a nun when I was a young girl. So I now believe in ghosts.

I only wish I had seen the Lady in White. I may have been able to console her. She only goes to stone houses, and whenever I see a stone house I always think of the Lady in White.

This is a true story.

The Ghost of the Alex

A jewel-box among the legitimate playhouses of North America, the Royal Alexandra Theatre impresses in the Beaux-Arts manner. The building was erected in 1906-07 and since then its stage has known all the leading actors and actresses of the time, touring companies and national theatres, as well as local productions like *Spring Thaw*.

The building was slated for demolition in 1963. But that year it was acquired by Edwin Mirvish, mechandiser, producer, and benefactor, who oversaw an extensive restoration to its Edwardian splendour. He and his son David Mirvish now operate it successfully. The same team once owned and operated the Old Vic in London, which has the tradition of being England's most haunted theatre.

Indeed, most playhouses are said to be haunted. But to my knowledge the first report of a haunting at the Royal Alex (as it is affectionately called) appeared in print in the *Toronto Star* in a Halloween column in 1994. Until then, the only thing that theatre-goers and ghost-hunters had for amusement was a passage in Robertson Davies's *Fifth Business* (1970), which vividly describes a magic show that takes place in the theatre. The performance of the magician Magnus Eisengrim is interrupted when a member of the audience, perhaps someone in a box, demands to know in a loud voice: "Who killed Boy Staunton?"

Here is the column from the *Star:*

Strange things go bump in the night at the Royal Alexandra Theatre.

Darrin Carter, 29, who operates the electronics board that controls the lighting for *Crazy for You*, claims to have seen a ghost a month ago.

"I was alone at my computer on the fourth floor fly rail, which is open to the stage so that I can look down on the actors," he recalled for "Screams & Whispers."

"It was dark except for my little reading light; I was reading a book. There is just one door to this fly rail and anyone going out would have to walk by me. Then, just before intermission, I saw a man from the neck down cross my field of vision above the top of my book, wearing a beige shirt and brown pants. I looked up. There was no one there and the door wasn't swinging shut. All the hair stood up on my arms and the back of my neck right until intermission."

Carter thinks he may have seen the ghost of a "flyman" who was accidentally killed at the theatre about twelve years ago. Another ghost said to haunt the place is that of a woman, a member of the audience, who died many years ago in the second balcony. "We've all had a feeling of a presence here," Carter says.

Did the experience terrify him? "I wasn't scared so much as exhilarated."

The Gibson-Atwood Ghost

Not far from Alliston there stands a farmhouse built in the 1860s. Over more than a century it has seen a lot of history. In the early 1970s it served as the home of two novelists, Graeme Gibson and Margaret Atwood, and a ghost.

In later years Gibson recalled how he was on the verge of sleep in the upstairs bedroom just before midnight on a cold winter night, when he heard something stirring downstairs.

⚬

It wasn't a noise I could immediately identify. Then I heard someone in the vestibule. Almost immediately there was the sound of footsteps on our stairs. These were not the creakings or groanings that haunt old houses, but the very specific and unmistakable noise of a woman's shoes as she ascended towards the back of the house.

Now it is important to emphasize several points. There had been no sound of a car on our curving drive, yet through my partially open window I could hear trucks half a mile away on Highway 89. Moreover, we'd recently acquired a stray Bluetick hound that insisted upon sleeping in a pile of hay in the drive shed. Max, as we'd named him, had proven himself a reassuring addition to our menagerie by baying alarums at every provocation — both real and imagined. Yet he'd made not a whimper. To top it off we'd had the locks changed; only Margaret and I had keys and she was miles away.

And yet there was a woman in my house wearing solid shoes. I called, "Hello!" in the darkness. "Who's that?" I heard her reach the small window at the top of the stairs; then she began walking along the hall towards my bedroom door. She walked methodically, or so it seemed to me, with a kind of comfortable assurance in the dark, as if she was familiar with the house. Again I called out but there was no answer. Only the clear sound of heels on the pine floorboards.

In retrospect, I believe I remained in my bed out of puzzlement. If it had been a man's shoes I'd heard I'd have been more immediately apprehensive, and therefore self-protective. As it was, I left it too late. She was almost at the door when it came to me with a genuine shiver (as if someone were walking on my grave?) that it was a ghost....

We had no bedside lamp, so the only light switch was on the wall beside the door, which opened towards me and was ajar. In order to turn on the light I'd have to reach past eight or ten inches of dark space that contained whatever it was that waited out there. I'd like to say that I did so, that I went over to see who or what she was. But I didn't. In some fundamental way I didn't want to know.

So I lay there while assuring myself that she could have no quarrel with me. We had not been in the house long enough. Anyway, try as I might, I could remember no instance of a so-called spirit actually harming anyone. Eventually I went to sleep.

I told Margaret, of course. But as time passed we forgot about it, as one does. Perhaps I was melodramatic in my response to the sounds of the old house. Perhaps I'd drunk more than I'd thought; perhaps, as Scrooge protested, it was merely a scrap of undigested mutton. Certainly, without confirmation that would have been the end of it.

Almost two years later we arranged with a new-found friend to mind the house while we went north for our annual escape into the bush. We had not told her about our 'ghost,' nor to my knowledge had we told anyone she might have known. Certainly she had no recollection of the story.

On our return we discovered that our friend had been visited not once, but three times, exactly as it had happened to me. The noise in the vestibule, the sound of footsteps on the stairs, and then in the hall. The alarming difference, for her, was that she took the footsteps to be those of a man. She didn't open the door either. Instead, she threw herself against it to keep him out. But there had been no attempt to enter.

After moving back to Toronto, we had a series of tenants before finally selling the farm. Each lasted for about a year before moving on. One day when I was visiting the second family — they were from Northern Ireland — the woman said, "Tell us about the ghost." I asked her to tell me first, whereupon she reported that her husband had been wakened by a woman who seemed to walk past him into a small room behind the bedroom. At first he'd thought it was his wife but immediately discovered she was still asleep beside him. Their bed was placed as ours had been, so whatever it was had apparently entered the room through the doorway from the hall.

A married daughter was coming to visit and they had put a child's crib in the back room because it had logically seemed to be a nursery of some kind. We all wondered if it was the crib that had encouraged, permitted, or whatever, the "spirit" to actually enter the bedroom.

After that there were a number of incidents that are harder to verify. She appeared at least once again, and they were all convinced, for example, that the covers and pillows in the crib were moved about and some stuffed toys were rearranged.

And then, about four years later, we met, once more, a young woman who had lived in our house as a mother's helper for almost a year. She told us that she had actually seen the woman from her bedroom, which opened onto the hall at the top of the stairs. She says she called out, "Hey, can I help you?" Neither young nor old, and wearing a plain, vaguely archaic blue dress, the apparition had seemed to pause, and then continued along the hall. There had been a great sadness about her. Our young friend hadn't said anything, at the time, because she feared we'd think she was nuts, or a witch, and she needed the work.

While the unconfirmed episodes give convincing substance to this story, it has been the repetition of an almost identical experience that has forced me to believe that some ghostly phenomenon really was outside my door that night....

A Very Strange Experience

From time to time, some people report, the experience of the reality of the world seems to wax and wane. It recedes from their senses and memories. It does not always return. Familiar things take on a curiously unfamiliar aspect; unfamiliar things assume a surprisingly familiar form. Such experiences are quite striking and unsettling and make a strong impression on memory. Psychiatrists, observing elements of dissociation, speak of the condition they called *derealization*. Psychologists, noting the ability of memory to knit the factual and the fictitious into a seamless whole, refer to *confabulation*. Parapsychologists are free to talk about altered states of consciousness and other dimensions of reality.

Here is one account of the familiar becoming unfamiliar — or the unfamiliar becoming familiar. It was written for me by Edith Fowke in October 1989, and it refers to her experience in England in August of that year. At the time of her death a few years later, Edith Fowke was the country's ranking folklorist. Her mentor was Marius Barbeau and her friend was Helen Creighton. She was especially knowledgeable about folksongs, which she collected in a scholarly manner and published in popular collections, and in later years she began to interest herself in narratives of legends and urban lore. Fowke was a matter-of-fact person, unlike Creighton who had a "sixth sense" and admitted to unusual experiences. This disorienting experience puzzled Fowke in her latter years.

Last summer I had a very strange experience. I was going to a festival in England, and needed to reserve a room before I left Canada. The festival was being held in the seaside town of Sidmouth, which is quite small and very popular so hotels tend to fill up early.

I phoned the festival office and asked them to see if they could find a room for me, saying I would phone again the next day. When I called the second time I was told that the Devoran Hotel had a cancellation and that I should phone Mrs. Clifford at Sidmouth 3151. I said that was fine because I'd stayed at the Devoran the year before and had liked it. Accordingly I phoned the number and booked for the week. When I mentioned that I had stayed there for a few days the previous summer, Mrs. Clifford said I hadn't, because she booked only by the week.

When I got to London I took a train from Paddington to Honiton, the railway station closest to Sidmouth, and got a taxi there, telling the driver to take me to the Devoran Hotel. When we reached Sidmouth I remembered the hotel's location and directed the driver to it. When we got there, it looked just as I remembered it. However, when I went in I didn't recognize Mrs. Clifford. Thinking that the hotel might have changed hands, I asked how long she had been there and she told me fifteen years. I then noticed some differences to what I remembered. The desk was placed at right angles to the front door while I remembered it as being parallel last year. The dining-room was on the opposite side of the front hall to what I remembered. However, the location was just as I remembered, and when I started going to the various festival programs I knew exactly how to reach them from the Devoran. The whole block was familiar to me, and there was no other hotel in it that looked enough like the Devoran for me to think that that was where I had stayed.

Another strange point was that the previous year the festival office had given me a phone number to book a room, saying it was for the Elizabeth Hotel. I had called and made my booking, but when, on reaching the town, I went to the Elizabeth Hotel, which was at the corner of a block, they had no record of my booking. I showed the clerk the phone number I had been given and he said it might be for the Devoran, which was right next door. I went into the Devoran, and they had my reservation. The confusion over the phone number and hotel name apparently resulted from the fact that the Devoran and the Elizabeth were together on the festival office's alphabetical listing. If my memory was wrong on this point, it might have been the Elizabeth Hotel I stayed at the previous year. However, it was considerably larger than the Devoran: I remembered it, but it didn't seem to me that I had stayed there.

This confusion naturally puzzled me, and during the week I was there I tried to think of some explanation. I looked at all the hotels in the block where I knew I had stayed, and none except the Devoran looked familiar. When I came home I looked to see if I had kept my receipt from the previous year, but I hadn't. Thus, this experience remains a mystery to me.

The Sticky Man

Donna Schillaci, a mother who lives in Oakville, Ontario, saw my letter in a local newspaper inviting readers to send me their true-life "ghost stories."

Ms. Schillaci had a scary experience to relate, one that involved not only herself but also her young son Adam. She sent me one account of "the sticky man" on June 5, 1990, and then, on June 22, 1990, a second, fuller account. It is the second account that is being reproduced here.

One cannot help but wonder: is there a "sticky man" in the basement of her house? Is the spirit there still, biding time until the appropriate moment when it will reappear?

June 22, 1990

Dear Mr. Colombo,

As I'm writing this letter to you I can't help but wonder if anyone could possibly understand or even believe what both my small son Adam and I experienced. But I guess that's what you want to hear about.

About a year and a half ago, when Adam was almost two years old, we moved into an older house. I think the house was between eighty and ninety years old. I never felt anything unusual about the house when we first moved in, but as time went on I felt a heaviness about the walls. I ignored the feeling.

Then one day, while in the basement, I felt the heaviness again. It was stronger this time. I noticed the furnace room door was more open than usual. Perhaps in vacuuming I had bumped into it. I couldn't remember.

And then I saw it — its form transparent so I could see the bricks of the wall through it. What caught my eye most of all was the figure's face. It was male. His eyes were leering and devilishly playful. He seemed to be challenging me — and in a frightening way.

I ran back upstairs as fast as I could. I tried to pretend I had imagined it all. It was hard. The bathroom, the shower, the tub were all down there in the basement, and when I went down there I had to feel comfortable.

Thereafter, as much as possible, I tried to keep the furnace room door closed. Some days I felt something in there, other days nothing. Gradually I began to forget about it all.

Then one day, while I was showering in the basement, Adam screamed from outside the shower curtains. It was a horrible scream, one I had never heard from him before. I shakingly opened the curtain and asked him what was wrong. He screamed, "Mommy, a sticky man on the wall!"

I quickly climbed out of the tub, looked around, and tried as best I could to see something where he pointed with his tiny finger. There was nothing there. He kept saying, "Sticky man, sticky man!" Instead of asking Adam too many questions, I knelt beside him and told him it was all pretend. He calmed down.

The first time this happened my explanation was enough. Yet it happened two more times. And always it was a "sticky man" he saw. Early one evening Adam was dancing in the kitchen. He got strangely delirious with joy and laughter. With both arms waving to the music he loudly cried out, "Sticky man is coming upstairs!"

Frightened, I yelled out powerfully for the "sticky man" to go back downstairs and to leave us alone. I ranted, raged, and repeatedly stamped my feet at the edge of the basement steps. I stated it wasn't fair. He was frightening a little child. I never let on he was scaring the skin off my face, too.

From that evening on, we were no longer bothered by his appearances. And if I did "feel" him around, I bravely and confidently spoke out. My commands were simple. Go away. Sometimes my tone would soften and I would pray for this poor soul to find its way back to God because I instinctively sensed he was lost. But I always made it very clear — I didn't want him around.

I try not to talk to Adam about his experiences. I have to admit I'd love to know how much he does remember. Six months ago he asked if mommy remembered the "sticky man." A jolt of panic sped up my spine. I looked sadly into his clear hazel eyes, quickly nodded yes, and changed the subject. I don't want him to be afraid of life, and I don't want him believing in ghosts. I'm firm about that. Yet it's too late. He's constantly zapping ghosts with an imaginary gun. Maybe he's lucky: he hasn't associated "sticky man" with ghosts. I really don't know.

As for myself, I still feel my stomach turn whenever I talk about it. No matter how much courage I mustered up in facing it, there was always fear not far behind. But I have to admit I'm stronger for having stood up to a ... can I say it? A ghost!

Sincerely,
Donna Schillaci

The Vision of a Crime

This is an account of a haunting with a difference. Is it possible for someone who is living today to "tune in" to the events of the past and witness them as they unfold? Mediums and psychics claim to have this power — the ability to be "sensitive" to the past. They maintain that the past, far from being "dead," is very much "alive."

This account was sent to me by Allen Goldenthal, B.Sc., D.V.M., in response to a request in the *Toronto Sun* for accounts of the paranormal. Dr. Goldenthal is a veterinarian and remains as puzzled by his experience as the day he sent me this letter, June 9, 1987. This is a very vivid account of a vision of a crime that remains unsolved.

~~~

I read with interest your request in the *Sunday Sun* for people with any insight into psychic phenomena to share this information with you.

If I had seen this request a year ago, I would have ignored it completely, as I was made to feel apprehensive about revealing something of the strange, unnatural events that have occurred to me over the years. In the past I shared these stories only with the closest of friends, and even some of them were quite skeptical about them. Regardless of that, one event left me more relaxed and free to talk of my psychic experiences.

In January of 1987, I was driving north up Warden Avenue towards Highway 7. Suddenly, up ahead, on the west side of the road, a southbound car pulled over. It was an old car, lime to faded green in colour. The driver of the car was a man. A woman got out of the car, pulling a child behind her. The woman was about six feet tall. She had a build that was almost masculine. She wore a long black dress and a high collar. The dress went down to her ankles. She had silver-platinum hair, a high-up hairdo, done in a fifties style.

At first I thought she was taking the child into the field to pee. But then I noticed the child struggling and trying to pull away. The child's hair was cut short, almost in what they used to call a Prince Valiant hairstyle. I placed the child between four and six years of age. Then the woman started dragging the child across the road to the field on the east side. I could hear the child yelling for help, even though my windows were up. At one point she paused in the centre of the road and looked directly at me. Even though I was in the northbound lane doing seventy km per hour, I did not seem to be getting any closer to her. It began to bother me that the cars in the southbound lane were passing by this scene as if nothing was happening.

When I came alongside the parked car, the man in the driver's seat turned to face me. He was Greek or Italian in appearance, with an oblong head, full moustache, and balding pate. His eyes were dark and cold.

Finally I had driven past the scene. I was about fifty yards down the road when the strangeness of everything suddenly dawned on me. I turned the car around and stopped. There was no one there and no longer any car. Then the name of the car — BelAir or Belmont — suddenly hit me. I don't know why, because I am not at all familiar with these automobiles.

The next day I related what had happened to me to some friends and inquired of them what I should do. Their reply was that if I had witnessed a crime I could expect to read about it in the papers in a day or so and then I could give my information to the police. Obviously nothing had happened, or at least nothing had appeared in the newspapers, so I stored the scene in my mind. I could no longer sleep well at night, however, as I was troubled by the events I had witnessed.

It dawned on me that what I had witnessed might have occurred in the past, long ago. Nevertheless I refused to tell anyone else about the vision, even though it weighed heavily on my mind. There is a certain amount of fear connected with talking about such things. As a public servant, I have to consider what my clients' reactions would be if I talked about such things. So I kept quiet about it for four months. By April I knew that I would no longer be at peace with myself unless I investigated the matter more fully. So I resolved to act.

One of my clients was a constable with 41 Division, as I remember. I asked him to do me a favour and investigate the first vision for me. I told him I believed that it took place in the time period between 1956 and 1960, that some crime or other was committed farther into the field on the east side, and that I believed the child was a boy between four and six years old.

Constable Adams did some inquiring for me and got back to me a few days later. He had created quite a stir because the oldest officer in York Region had only had twenty-five years of service on the force. But the officer did recall coming onto the force with an unsolved murder in the files. My client protected my interests by not telling him why he was interested in this case and where he had received his information about it until he had talked to me.

The facts of the case are these. On January 9, 1955, young Judy Carter was abducted from her Toronto home on Sherbourne Street and taken to Warden and Highway 7 where she was murdered. She was six years old. Her body was found on January 11 beside the creek that at one time flowed past Warden which, at that time, was only a concession road. Somehow I had witnessed a crime that had occurred four months before I was even born! The Chief of Police for York who investigated the crime was Harvey Carps and he retired without ever closing the case. Constable Adams informed Metro Homicide that I was willing to talk about the case I had seen. He told me that they would call me in the future for what information I could give. But that was some time ago. I'm still waiting, but at least I can sleep at night.

"Betty Louty"

Here is a well-told account of an experience that seems incredible. It was written by Jo Atkins, a writer in Willowdale, Ontario. She assured me that every word of it is true.

When Elizabeth was small "Betty Louty" appeared as an imaginary playmate. She came every afternoon for a friendly visit. We arranged the coffee table for Betty's visit: lace tea cloth, tiny cups and saucers, cream and sugar, and the inevitable cookies were part of the ritual. Elizabeth held her one-sided, polite, somewhat comforting conversations with her unseen guest and played the sympathetic friend. Before my older child was due home Betty Louty would depart.

"Where does Betty live?" I asked.

"A long way away," was the only answer I ever got.

No one in our family knew anyone by that name. It was unusual and we often wondered what had prompted Elizabeth to invent it. We put it down to the vivid imagination of a creative high-strung child who had suddenly found herself without her closest friend and ally ... her sister.

A few years later we all went to Jamaica for a holiday. In Kingston, a visit to the famous straw market was mandatory, as they each wanted a doll, dressed colourfully in the traditional costume, balancing a basket of fruit on its head.

Our older girl chose a doll from the first stall in the market. But not Elizabeth. She moved from stall to stall but did not find a doll she wanted. No! No! was all we heard. We became a little fractious. She became more determined.

"I want that one," Elizabeth said finally, pointing most definitely in the direction of the farthest corner of the top row of dolls.

"Take one from the bottom row," I said. "They're all the same." The heat in the market and the intractability of my daughter were getting to me.

"I want that one," she insisted, still pointing.

The old lady moved her pole along the row, first to one doll, then to the next. She turned to look at me.

"They are not all the same. Each one is signed by the person who made it," she said reproachfully.

"That's her!" said Elizabeth suddenly, eyes alight.

With a great deal of patience the old lady hooked the doll down for her. She patted the child on the head.

"This one is made for you, darlin'. This lady is not makin' dolls any more. This is the last one she made. She's been waitin' here for you."

"I know she's special. I'll look after her," said Elizabeth as she hugged the doll tightly and covered her with kisses.

Throughout our holiday, that doll never left Elizabeth's side. She slept, ate, walked with her, and would prop her gently on the sand before going into the water.

"She would like to swim, too, but she's afraid of the currents in the water," said our young one.

"Currants are in cake," I said jokingly. How could she possibly have known about ocean currents since she was so young and not familiar with the seashore?

"She's tired and needs a nap," Elizabeth announced as soon as we returned home.

"I think you do, too," I said. "Why don't you undress her and get her ready for bed?"

It was so quiet in Elizabeth's room, I thought she must have fallen asleep, but when I peeped in I found the doll had been carefully undressed by my little girl. She had taken off all the clothes and had only the bare ragdoll in her hands, cradling it gently as if it were a newborn child.

"Your bath's ready but you can't put your doll in with you. She'll get too wet," I said.

"She's afraid of water. She told me so," said Elizabeth very defensively. This game was getting to be too much for me!

"Well, let's pick up your clothes anyway," I said. "After your bath you can put her clothes back on."

As I picked up the clothes, I remembered the old lady in the Kingston market. I could not see the signature of the maker. Good saleswoman, I thought!

"I wonder who made this doll," I said.

"Betty. It's writing; I can't read it," said Elizabeth as she handed me the doll's apron.

There, on the inside band, was the maker's name ... "Betty Louty."

The imaginary playmate never appeared after that holiday in Jamaica. My daughter has her own home now but she still has the doll. For all these years she has treasured her.

It seems that "Betty Louty" finally came home.

Apparition of a Cat

Pet lovers in general and cat fanciers in particular will appreciate the following account. It tells of the crisis apparition of the family cat.

I received the following letter from T.J. Muckle, M.D., F.R.C.P.(C.), Director of Laboratories, Chedoke Division, Chedoke-McMaster Hospitals, Hamilton, Ontario. It was dated December 20, 1988, and was written to me in response to an interview on CHUM-FM about the supernatural and the paranormal.

In the summer of 1976, I took my wife and three girl children to Camp Oconto on Eagle Lake, northwest of Kingston, for a vacation (for them) and a working holiday (for me). I was the "camp doctor."

In the middle of the afternoon, several days later, I was sitting in an easy chair, reading a book on the verandah of our small bungalow. The chair was sideways-on, so that in the corner of my eye I could see the living-room through the open door. Quiet suddenly, but at the same time with no sense of dramatic suddenness, I could see our pet cat walking slowly across the room, apparently quite unconcerned, calmly looking straight ahead. It took me a couple of seconds to realize that she was walking along a foot and a half or so above the floor level. She ambled across to the other side of the room and, just short of the far wall, disappeared — not quite instantly, but within a fraction of a second.

This "apparition" had been present, I suppose, for about fifteen seconds. I would like to emphasize, however, that there was nothing about what I saw to suggest any form of apparition. The cat was normal in every detail, completely opaque and moving in her accustomed fashion. She was not surrounded by any dark aura, or glow, and I have to say that in every way, apart from being a foot and a half off the floor, appeared absolutely normal. At the time of the "apparition" I had no sense of dread, or fear, no sensation of cold or heat, or any other unusual sensation whatsoever.

My first thought within a second or so of her appearing, was the following: how did she manage to travel all the way from Hamilton? Then I realized that she was, in fact, a foot and a half off the floor, and it couldn't be her. By this time she was about one-third of the way across the room, and for the remainder of her walk I just watched her with my mind blank. My sense of blankness persisted for maybe a minute or so after she had disappeared. Then I began to "re-run the tapes," and take a closer look at the living-room to see if, by any faint chance, it could have been some sort of optical illusion and that a cat very like ours had in fact been walking on something that I hadn't perceived. However, I couldn't find anything to substantiate this.

I called two of my children from nearby to tell them what I had seen and to give me a hand to see if we could find any cat anywhere in or near the bungalow, just in case I was losing my mind. We couldn't. During this exercise I began to wonder not whether or how I had seen this, but why. Immediately, of course, I was reminded of having read of similar sightings and that the associations were usually bad. Half an hour later, telling my wife and my other children of the occurrence, the only strong impression I had of the whole event was a feeling of the absolute reality of this "apparition."

The above is strange enough in itself, but the real impact came about two and a half hours later, when we went into supper and I was told that there had been a telephone message for me at the Camp

Telephone Office from our neighbours in Hamilton. I went across and, on the way, the uneasy suspicion that something bad had indeed happened recurred. I telephoned our neighbour, and she told me that our cat had been run over by a car about three hours before, which was pretty near the time I saw the "apparition." She also added that the cat had not been killed instantly but had lived for a few minutes after being hit. I immediately wondered whether I would have seen the apparition had the cat died instantly — the implication, I trust, is obvious.

This is the only experience that I have had that I would really call paranormal, although I have had other experiences such as "some places give me the creeps," and on two occasions I have been overwhelmed by a fainting sensation when somebody nearby was, unbeknownst to me, in the process of fainting. Please feel free to use this experience as you wish.

Hunting Henry's Ghost

Some people's faces light up at the whisper of the word "ghosts." Other people's faces grow dim at the mention of spirits and spectres.

Kathryn Newman's face lights up when she hears the word "ghosts." She is a freelance journalist. She contacted me for any information I might have about ghosts in Toronto, especially those that might inhabit buildings in the city's west end.

As it happened, I was able to draw her attention to some reports of ghosts and hauntings in that quarter, one of the older parts of Metropolitan Toronto. She was able to use some of them in her survey of "local haunts." It appeared in the community newspaper *The Villager* and was called "Looking for Ghosts? They're Right in Your Backyard."

In her account she mentioned the haunting of the Royal Canadian Legion's Hall on Royal York Road, below the Queensway. It is believed that the ghost of a young soldier, named Henry, is trapped in the hundred-year-old building.

Kathryn was plainly attracted to the idea of Henry, so she decided to devote one night of her life to seeking him out. She did so and described the experience in a second, personal story that she called "A First-hand Encounter with Henry's Ghost."

Here is the personal story. May your face light up reading it!

Ghosts have always been a part of my life.

As a young child I would sit at my grandmother's knee and listen to her weave stories of haunted spectres and eerie happenings. At the end of each story, she would tell me that when you are dealing with ghosts, you have to be ready for the unexpected.

As a freelance writer, I have learned to expect the unexpected. However, no amount of stories, training, or experience could have ever prepared me for spending a night in "the haunted Legion Hall" on Royal York Road.

Originally the structure was built by Edward Stock and named Eden Court. The Stock family was one of the first families of settlers to populate the area that is now considered part of the Bloor West Village in the west end of Toronto. In its heyday the building was an attractive house with a sprawling porch, verandah and beautiful gardens.

There is a shadier side to the Stock House. During the 1930s it was used as a gambling hall and meeting place for the criminal element. Gangster Abe Orpen owned the building, and when it was renovated in 1966, bullet holes were found in the doors.

When Harry MacIsaac, the assistant steward at the Legion, informed me that permission had been granted for me to spend the night looking for the ghost of Henry, I almost jumped right out of my skin. The veterans and staff at the Legion had named the ghost Henry after a boarder who at one time resided in the attic.

I immediately recognized that I needed someone to accompany me on my adventure. It would have to be a person who could verify any ghostly phenomena and not jump to conclusions. My first and only choice was Sylvia Peda. She had a background in journalism, and we had worked together on many stories. Armed with notepads, a tape recorder, pens, talcum powder, and a flashlight with new batteries, we stepped through the Legion door into the unknown.

Bill Lazenby, president of Branch 217 Legion Hall, escorted us through the building and up onto the third floor. This was the floor that had the reputation of being the most haunted.

"There is something I should tell you. The light switch is at the end of the hall, and you have to walk down in darkness to turn it on. The only escape is by the main staircase. If you are cornered, you have had it."

Thankfully, the president turned on the switch for us and wished us luck. We were on our own.

Sylvia smiled one of the sly smiles that she is most famous for. With a gleam in her eye, she reminded me that we would probably be found with our heads at the bottom of the stairs, our faces frozen in hideous expressions of terror.

Despite Sylvia's bizarre sense of humour, I was glad that she was with me. I would not want to be in this place alone. Besides, when the atmosphere became too weird for my liking, I could always send Sylvia into the darkness to switch on the light.

We had to decide whether we wanted to conduct our investigations in the dark. After much discussion, we both decided that it might be wiser to leave the light on for the time being. While we were debating the issue of the light, we both became aware of a noticeable chill. It became intensely cold, and then Henry turned out the light. We tore down the stairs sensing Henry at our heels. It was then that I realized that I had left some of my equipment upstairs.

The second floor is set up as an entertainment area. Small tables are scattered along the side of the large room. At the back is a stage. We felt comfortable there. We convinced ourselves that we were safe and that nothing could happen on this floor. We relaxed.

We needed to gather our thoughts. "There is so much history here," Sylvia commented.

"Yes," I responded. "But it's more than that. When you think of what could have happened here with the gambling. Hey, maybe Henry's still up there in the wall," I chuckled uneasily.

There is a fine line between fantasy and reality. It was important to try to restrain my imagination. We needed facts, and we both knew it was time to go back upstairs and face Henry head on.

With courage and determination, we marched up the stairs. A ghostly green glow shone in the hall, and the doorway to the third floor was cloaked in darkness. Somewhere between the second and the third floor, I lost my courage. But it was my turn to brave the hall and turn the light on. I tried not to notice the room getting colder. I switched on the light and then I heard footsteps and thumping right behind me.

Sylvia sprinkled talcum powder on the floor, and we ran for our lives. This time I remembered my equipment. A cold breeze passed by us in the entrance on the second floor. We stood for a few seconds, trying to determine its direction, and then we returned to the safety of our table in the entertainment area.

Traditionally, the witching hour is the time when spirits are said to be most active. As the clock on the second floor ticked towards midnight, I wondered just how much more activity I could endure in one night.

For the next half hour we listened to the building creak and moan. Cold breezes invaded our space. Unusual noises and whispers were heard coming from the second-floor bar. I experienced itching on my hands and feet. It felt like I had been exposed to fiberglass.

Sylvia became so cold that she was forced to put her winter jacket on. Then, at 12:30 a.m., she was touched on the head by an unseen entity. It took her several seconds to recover from her encounter with the ghost.

We began to discuss our next move, and just as we were about to enter the stairway hall, the toilet on the third floor flushed by itself. Sylvia and I grabbed hold of each other's arms for support. We held our breath. "I didn't know ghosts went to the bathroom," Sylvia commented.

The hours ticked away. We began to discuss our departure. We had seen enough ghostly phenomena to last a lifetime, and we both sensed it was time to go. It was important to leave the building the way we found it. That meant all the lights in the building needed to be shut off.

For the last time we climbed the stairs to the third floor. I felt the ghost's presence ahead of me. I was not nervous. In fact, I sensed a sadness. Sylvia did not sense the same thing. Her sense was one of a spectre that was lost, caught between worlds.

White powder footsteps had formed in the talcum that we had sprinkled on the floor. The steps started on one side of the room, travelled in one direction, and stopped suddenly. I flipped the light off, and darted through the hallway, and down the stairs. I did not look back.

One by one we turned off lights until we reached the rear door of the second floor. That was the way out. I felt relieved to be outside the building. It was good to feel the cold fresh air. I turned, and waved goodbye to the upper back windows of the building. I knew somehow that Henry was watching us leave.

As I drove the car to the front of the building, I decided to stop to take a few pictures. Sylvia and I climbed out. I was fiddling with my camera, when a circular flash of blue light shone from behind the centre curtained window on the third floor. Several seconds later the curtains on the second floor parted ever so slightly.

Upon reflection, Sylvia and I both believe that this was Henry's way of saying goodbye. One thing is for certain. Whoever Henry is, he gave us an experience neither of us will ever forget.

Trick or treat.

The Most Beautiful Woman in the World

Robert Hoshowsky is a freelance writer who lives in Toronto. He had a most amazing experience. "The Most Beautiful Woman in the World" is his account of that experience. His story has all the qualities of imaginative fiction, yet the author maintains that it is a complete and accurate depiction of what he saw early one morning when he went out jogging in North Toronto. It first appeared in the October 1992 issue of the community weekly *Midtown Voice* — the Halloween issue.

A long time ago, before it became fashionable, I was a jogger. Not just a block or two, but five, ten, even fifteen *miles* each and every night. Initially, I was joined by friends. The three of us huffed and wheezed our way through the labyrinth of streets and alleyways known as North Toronto a couple of hours after dinner, long after the sun had dipped below the horizon and the food in our stomachs had settled enough so we wouldn't puke. With our lungs straining for the next breath, we savoured every second of our run with youthful enthusiasm.

After a while, however, one friend after another dropped off and sought other pursuits. Tyler discovered the joys of poker, and became forever lost to gambling away his pocket change after class. Dwight formed a heavy metal band, and pretended to bite the heads off stuffed parakeets in the high-school auditorium during lunch. Since I had no musical abilities whatsoever, I kept running, alone.

One night, feeling especially adventuresome, I decided to try twenty miles. No stopping, not for pain or traffic lights. This was in August, and there are surprisingly few people awake at three in the morning.

Dressed in a ratty old muscle shirt and shorts that looked like they'd been washed ten thousand times, I was ready. And, up until the time I saw her, I was having a pretty good run. She was about half a mile away, on the other side of the street. I rubbed the sweat from my eyes and kept on running. At first, I thought she was a dishevelled housewife, wandering around looking for her cat. That is, until I noticed a few little things.

Her bare feet weren't touching the ground.

I stopped so suddenly that I nearly fell flat on my face. The "housecoat" she was wearing was a nightgown, a very old-fashioned one, adorned with a high lace collar and white material that reached to her ankles. Her hair was loose, and hung around her slender shoulders in thick black ropes.

What shocked me the most was her body. It was translucent, not like anything I had seen before. With every passing second, sections of her appeared and disappeared at the same time. She seemed just as astonished to see me as I did her, looking at me like I was intruding on her territory. Yet she was striking, with firm, high cheekbones and a lovely oval face. She couldn't have been more than thirty.

Her entire appearance suggested nobility, as if she had just drifted off the canvas of a Pre-Raphaelite painting. Long, slender hands, the supple neck of a swan, and enormous dark eyes that seemed to occupy most of her exquisite face. I fell in love with her in an instant, despite the fact she was a ghost. Never before have I wished so hard for one thing: for this woman to be truly alive, with warm human flesh and the breath of the living, not the wind of the dead. By the way she was dressed, she had been that way for at least a hundred years.

As I walked towards her, I felt my knees turn to water and stopped, not out of fright but of fear — of myself. We stood on opposite sides of the road staring at one another for an eternity, a supernatural breeze blowing the nightgown around her naked form. She was trapped, a prisoner caught in the nether world between life and death; a place I could not enter, and a land she could never leave.

I turned and ran, stopping only when I reached the top of the hill. The instant I turned to look at her, she swirled around, her body slowly disappearing into the darkness. The look of sadness hadn't left her eyes, and won't until the day I am dead, when we can meet again, not as strangers, but lovers.

She was, and forever will be, the most beautiful woman I never met.

Short Circuit

By tradition, ghosts and spirits of the departed are associated with phantom footsteps, cold spots, creepy feelings, and other related phenomena. They are not widely associated with electromagnetic effects. Yet if the presence of a ghost can produce the sound of a footfall or a sudden drop in temperature, it should certainly be able to snap the thin filament of an electric light-bulb or upset the delicate operation of a facsimile machine.

Are there fifty light-bulbs in your house? If so, how often do the bulbs burn out? You will ponder such questions after reading Jack Kapica's account of odd and unusual experiences in the wake of the passing of a friend and tenant. The author of the account, a native of Montreal, is a long-time Toronto resident. He is a writer for the *Globe and Mail*, having served as its book editor and its religion columnist. He and his wife, the writer Eve Drobot, live in the Riverdale area of the city.

— ·ıı◄●◖▨◗●►ıı· · —

Losing Paul was more than losing a friend. It wasn't until he died that we realized we had lost a member of the family.

We had shared a home for seventeen years. We met when he was recovering from his second busted marriage, and he said he just wanted to learn how to live alone. No problem, I said, I wasn't looking for company, just someone to help carry the cost.

And so we worked out an arrangement. We shared a house and the entrance to the house, but Paul's rooms were discrete, as was his schedule. He worked as an editor at a newspaper, and started at three in the afternoon, and returned only after closing down the bars in the wee hours. When the front door slammed, we knew it had to be 1:35 a.m., which represented bar-closing hour plus a five-minute cab ride.

We never socialized actively. Sometimes, days would pass when we didn't see him, and we could tell he was at home only because the mail had been sorted. It wasn't until my wife found him stretched out on his bed, dead of a mercifully sudden heart attack at the age of fifty-three, that I realized he was like the brother you see twice a year, at Thanksgiving and Christmas, and whose company you enjoy so much you swear you've got to do this more often. But somehow you never do.

That awful day, we had to wait for several hours in the company of two policemen for the coroner to come by to declare that everything was as it appeared. Well, everything indeed was as it appeared to everyone but the cat, who over the years had developed a special relationship with Paul. He came up to Paul's room, jumped upon his bed, and curled up against his already cold body and began to purr.

Like many single men, Paul had simplified everything in his life, from his wardrobe (jeans) to his furniture (black leather) to his passions (the Blue Jays) to his diet (peanut butter, beer, and cigarettes). It was the diet that killed him two games into the 1993 American League Championship Series.

Over the years Paul often commented on how much he enjoyed our living arrangement. He even welcomed the arrival of my daughter who for the first five years of her life refused to sleep, and put up an all-night racket that anyone else would have found irritating. It was a "natural" sound, Paul said, and he liked it. She grew up calling him "Uncle" Paul.

His single-guy professional lifestyle allowed him to put a respectable amount of money in the bank, and friends were always suggesting he do something with it, such as invest in real estate. So on several occasions, he said, "Maybe I should buy a house of my own."

The thought of losing Paul to another house was very saddening. But my wife and I would always counter, "Oh, Paul, how would you manage? You can't even change a light-bulb."

That was a terrible mistake.

Because shortly after Paul died, the light-bulbs in the house started to blow.

In a house with something like fifty lights, a bulb is bound to burn out reasonably often. So when one of the three-bulb dining-room fixture lights burned out, I thought nothing of it. But the next day, the second one blew. Then the third went on the third day.

Then the fax machine went into permanent "receive" mode, as though someone were trying to send us a fax, but nothing was coming out. My wife brought it to the Mitsubishi people, who pronounced it healthy, and sent it home with a recommendation to discuss it with the phone company. A phone company repairman replaced all the wires leading to the fax, declared them in perfect running order, and recommended we talk to an electrician. The electrician plugged the fax into a different electrical outlet, and it worked.

But, my wife protested, it worked for more than a year in the old outlet. What happened?

He considered the old outlet. "Beats me," he said. "Maybe it's haunted."

In fact, my wife said, the fax machine had stopped working only when ... only when ... ah, well, when Paul died.

In the meantime, I had replaced two lights in the master bedroom, one in my daughter's room, the swing arm over the computer, both vanities in the bathroom, both carriage lamps at the front door, the trilight in the study, two potlights in the basement, and the hanging one in the kitchen, which is such a bitch to change because of the glass bowl and the three set-screws holding it on to a swinging chain.

Just to add a menacing note, the microwave oven ceased working in the middle of a casserole, and the videotape recorder refused to record the Mighty Morphin' Power Rangers, which our daughter announced was going too far.

All in about four weeks. The situation had moved from coincidence to freakish unlikelihood.

One night, my wife, my daughter, and I lit a candle, held hands in a circle around it, and had a little chat with Paul.

We tried, as best we could, to explain that we all loved him dearly. He was not to worry, because the Blue Jays had won both the ALCS as well as the World Series. He was perfectly welcome in our home even if he was in no state to help with the rent. And we were terribly sorry we had ever teased him about the light-bulbs, so could he give our wiring a break, please?

Our daughter was convinced her parents had taken leave of their senses, but played along anyway. And a good thing, too — that very night, lights started to burn out at a rate much more statistically acceptable. I can't tell you what statistically acceptable means, but anyone who has lived in a home for a long time just knows the life rhythm of its light-bulbs.

The cat, however, was having none of it. He moved into Paul's room to await Paul's return.

Soon after, we started to plan a Christmas vacation, and contacted a woman called Diana, who is a genius at organizing other people's lives. She had helped us stage a reception at our house for Paul's friends and relatives after the funeral. We wanted Diana to take care of the house while we were away.

"Do I actually have to sleep there?" she asked.

Well, no, not if it's a problem, we said, but why?

"Because I don't want to stay over if Paul's going to be there."

I beg your pardon?

"I mean, he was there at his funeral party. I saw him there."

You sure it wasn't his brother? They look awfully alike.

"No, I know Paul, and it was Paul."

Okay, so it was Paul. And what was he doing?

"Oh, just walking around. He was picking up things and looking at them, then putting them down. He looked all right."

Okay, no sleep-overs. Just make sure the cat is fed and the plants watered.

A little later, I was talking on the phone to the information officer of the Anglican Church of Canada, when the other line rang. It was Diana, finalizing our arrangements for the holiday, and seeking more assurances that the electrical phenomena had stopped. As far as I could tell, they had, I said. And you still don't need to sleep over.

Back on the phone with the Anglicans, I told the information officer about that conversation, and about Paul and the light-bulbs. I mentioned the VCR and the microwave, too.

"Uh," he said, "we, ah, have some people here who could help you get rid of that sort of thing, if you want...."

Had it come to that, then? Bell, book, and candle? Were we going to hurl the wrath of heaven at Paul? I mean, were we going to petition the Almighty to cast our former tenant into eternal eviction just for trashing light-bulbs?

"Jeez, no," I said. "Thanks, but no. It would be just devastating to the cat."

"Oh," he said. "I understand."

I'm not sure he did.

PRAIRIES

The White Horse

The statue of a sparkling white horse stands twelve feet high at St. François Xavier on the Trans-Canada Highway west of Winnipeg. This is the story behind that statue.

In the 1690s, there lived a Cree chief with a beautiful daughter. She was so beautiful that not one but two Indian braves sought her hand. One was a Cree chief from Lake Winnipegosis and the other was a Sioux chief from Devil's Lake. The Cree was favoured because he had offered the daughter's father a beautiful pure white horse, a Blanc Diablo from Mexico. The prospect of such a gift was irresistible and the father succumbed.

So the favoured suitor presented his prospective father-in-law with the white horse and claimed his prize. This did not sit well with the rejected suitor, who summoned an escort of Sioux warriors and was seen thundering across the plains. Everyone fled. Quickly the suitor helped his bride mount the white horse. He leapt onto his grey steed, and they rode furiously westward, with the Sioux and his party in hot pursuit.

Despite its speed and endurance, the white horse became the undoing of the fleeing couple. They doubled back to mislead their pursuers and hid in the prairie bluffs, but once they were again on the open plain, the white horse was a mark that betrayed them. Finally, at a point just east of the present town of St. François Xavier, Sioux arrows killed the young couple. The suitor's grey mount was caught but the daughter's white horse escaped. Because the Crees believed the soul of the chief's daughter had passed into its body, they feared to approach the horse. It roamed the plains for years. It was never caught. So the prairie here is known as the White Horse Plain.

Eventually the belief grew that the ghostly form of the white horse would haunt the plain forever. It may be seen to this day. Today the spirit of the chief's daughter takes the form of the statue of the sparkling white horse.

Spirit of White Eagle

The Stony Indians live on three reserves near the town of Morley, northwest of Calgary. Common to the three reserves is the legend of the Spirit of White Eagle.

At certain times of the year, if one knows where to look, one may behold the spirit of White Eagle wearing his flowing white robes, astride his great white stallion, followed by his white dog.

He emerges from the mist on the peaks of the Ghost Hills and progresses majestically alongside the shores of Ghost Lake and Ghost River, disappearing into the heart of Devil's Head Mountain.

There is a reason for the vision of White Eagle. It seems this great chief led his Stony people to safety and prosperity in the Morley area following their humiliating defeat on the plains at the hands of the Cree and Blackfoot. Yet White Eagle privately yearned for revenge and found it when the traditional enemies attacked the Stony Indians in their mountainous stronghold. In the battle, White Eagle was wounded, but as he lay dying, he instructed his warriors to bury him at the peak of Devil's Head Mountain. They followed his dying wishes and as they did so they accidentally loosened some of the boulders at the peak. The attacking warriors were caught in the avalanche and killed. Thus did White Eagle die avenged. His ghost continues to patrol the hills and shores of the lake and river and the peak of Devil's Head Mountain to this day.

Who Calls?

There is a Cree legend about love and loss set in the beautiful valley of the Qu'Appelle River in Saskatchewan. The river flows west of Regina through a valley renowned for its echoes and reverberations.

The story is told of a Cree brave who paddled his birch-bark canoe through the river valley at night to the Cree village to claim as his bride a beautiful young woman.

In the darkness he heard a young woman's voice utter his name.

"Qu'appelle?" he cried out. "Who calls?"

There was no answer.

Then he heard the voice utter his name again.

"Who calls?"

There was no answer.

When he reached the Cree village, he learned to his sorrow that the beautiful young woman had died during the night.

Her dying words were his name.

Ever since that night, travellers on the river, when they listen attentively, may hear the voice of the Cree brave crying out, "Who calls?"

The Vanishing Village

Can an Indian village appear and disappear?

Sir Cecil Edward Denny was an original member of the North-West Mounted Police. He joined in 1874 and resigned in 1881 to become an Indian agent and archivist. A most peculiar incident occurred to him while he was stationed at Fort Walsh in the Cypress Hills area of Saskatchewan. He saw an Indian village appear and disappear.

The deeply puzzling incident occurred about four o'clock one afternoon in the summer of 1875. He was boating on the Oldman River about twenty-four kilometres from Fort Walsh when he was overtaken by a fierce storm and strong winds. Amid the sudden lightning and thunder, he beached his boat to wait out the storm. During a lull he could hear in the distance the rhythm of drums and the familiar chanting of Indians, "Hi-ya, hi-ya, hi-ya-ya." He staggered through the rain and wind towards the sounds. In the distance he could dimly discern a camp of teepees. The Cree

145

Indians were in a circle about a hundred yards away, brightly coloured, as if illuminated by the sun. Not only were there teepees but there were also Cree men and women moving about as if unaffected by the storm with its wind, thunder, and lightning.

"I congratulated myself upon meeting with an Indian camp where I could take shelter from such a storm. I concluded that this was the camp I had been told had gone up the river. I therefore landed and drew up the boat into the bush, tying it securely, and, taking my gun, made as quickly as possible through the wood toward the point from which the sounds could now be heard. The storm had now come down worse than ever, and the lightning was almost blinding. I made my way through the timber as fast as possible, it not being any too safe in such close proximity to the trees, and coming out into an open glade of quite an extent, I saw before me the Indian camp not more than two hundred yards away."

As he approached the settlement, he saw men and women and children moving about among the lodges. "What struck me as strange was the fact that the fires in the centre of many of the tents shone through the entrances, which were open."

He found himself engulfed in a cocoon of a flickering, bluish flame. Then he was hurled to the ground, senseless. He had to lie there, helplessly, while the storm raged. When it abated he rose to his feet and staggered in the direction of the village, only to find that it had vanished. He examined the ground as well as he could but he could find in the immediate vicinity no traces of any encampment.

Denny was badly shaken. The storm resumed its fury so he left his boat where it was and walked back to Fort Walsh, arriving there around midnight, exhausted. The next day he returned to the site of the vanished village. Again he found no signs of recent habitation, but this time in the clear weather he could discern a few rings of stone overgrown with grass where there had once been an encampment. He also found bleached human bones scattered about. From his guide he learned that there had once been a Cree village there that had been sacked and burned by the Blackfoot, who slaughtered every last inhabitant.

Frog Lake Vision

If you check books of Western history for Frog Lake, you will find an account of a dreadful massacre that took place there in 1885. What you will not find is any account of the vision that followed the massacre.

On April 2, 1885, a party of Crees, inspired by Métis leader Louis Riel, massacred most of the settlers at Frog Lake, a small community that lies in the valley between the North and South Saskatchewan Rivers. The Crees took two young women as hostages and forced them to accompany the band as it moved from one campsite to another to escape the avenging Canadian militia soldiers.

The two women were both named Theresa. One was Theresa Gowanlock, who was nineteen years old at the time. Somewhat older was her married friend, Theresa Delaney. They were held captive for eight weeks in all. A vision contributed to their safe release. Here is how it came about.

The Indian Reserve near Onion Lake, west of Fort Pitt, was the setting for the events prior to the massacre. In late March, the Cree leaders met here and demanded open rebellion against the white settlers and the militia. Big Bear cautioned against an uprising. The pow-wow was joined by a fat old woman with unkempt black hair who uttered a series of incantations and went into a trance. She, too, cautioned against rebellion. She explained, "No brave can move fast enough to outrun the soldiers who have a thousand bullets for every Indian brave."

The situation was unstable. A few days later, on the morning of April 2, the warriors surrounded the homestead of John Delaney. They took ten captives, including Theresa Gowanlock, and led them to the little church at Frog Lake, where two priests, conducting mass, quickly concluded the divine service. Then the warriors murdered all the male prisoners, including the two priests. Theresa Gowanlock and Theresa Delaney, wife of settler John Delaney, were spared to watch the mutilation of the bodies. The settlement was looted and the church was set on fire.

The two women captives were taken to Onion Lake where the old woman appeared again, Cassandra-like, to predict that no good would come of the rebellion. Fearful of the militia's revenge, the Cree took to the country, dragging their two captives with them. Even in retreat the old woman would not keep quiet but predicted destruction. Big Bear ordered her killed. She was dragged into the bushes and axed to death, her body being left for the wolves.

In late May the Cree were still on the run. One cloudy morning, Theresa Gowanlock reported that the Cree observed the clouds part and an image of the little church of Frog Lake appear in the sky. The church was observed to burst into flame. A rider on a white horse galloped up to the flaming church and dismounted, stretching out his hand as if to bless the fiery church. Then the clouds closed over the vision.

"We are doomed," Big Bear cried out. He was willing to trust the vision but not the words of the old woman. "Our world of beauty has vanished forever." The warriors began to quarrel and threaten one another. They were heedless of the approaching militia. Two days later they were surrounded by the militia at Frenchman's Butte. Some warriors fled, others were killed. Big Bear surrendered in July and was tried and sentenced to two years' imprisonment. He died almost immediately upon his release, his life no doubt shortened by the vision of the burning church.

The Travelling Ghost

Ghosts are usually rooted in rooms, houses, or regions of the country. But sometimes they travel from country to country. There are even globe-trotting ghosts!

Here is an account of a ghost that travelled over a great distance, from Iceland to Manitoba, and also through the passage of years. The Travelling Ghost is not a crisis apparition, like the Wynyard Apparition, which appeared at the moment of death. Instead, the Travelling Ghost is like a guardian angel or a mother who watches over her child, in this instance, a grown woman.

The story was told by Mrs. Herdis Eiriksson of Wawanesa, Manitoba. It was collected and translated from the Icelandic by Magnus Einarsson, who gives Mrs. Eiriksson's description of her mother's ghost: "She was wearing a dark skirt, exactly like — she was dressed as women generally were in their homes, in a dark skirt with a plaid apron and a greyish jacket with a white kerchief on her head. And she had ... four long braids, two on each side, that had been pinned up and hung down to the chest on either side."

Here is Mrs. Eiriksson's story in her own words.

During the spring of 1920 I became ill with typhoid fever, lay ill for a whole month. And then I was coming around, was up and about for two days, but then I got sick again and was much sicker than I had been before. The physician who attended me, Doctor Jackson, called in a physician, some specialist from Brandon, Manitoba, but Wawanesa is only thirty miles from Brandon. And also I had a nurse, a trained one. After the physicians had examined me they agreed that I had a malignancy; I had to be opened up, and the physician from Brandon said it was best if I were moved to Brandon as quickly as possible. And then they left me for a number of hours, the physicians and the nurse, and I was alone there.

This room was upstairs, window facing south, and the sun shone through the window. But after they were gone, I was gripped with such terrible anxiety that I started crying. I felt as sick as I was, having been sick for so long, and had become so thin, and that if I had to undergo an operation I would never survive it.

And when I am thinking about this, and completely — I felt I was totally succumbing to fatigue, I see all of a sudden where, out from the corner by the outer wall, I see where a woman comes, walking across the floor.... This woman comes there, walks over to the bed, lifts up the bedding, and then lifts up my nightgown, and places her hand on the spot where the physician had said he had found this sore, or whatever it was, and — and says in Icelandic (but, of course, I had been thinking in English, because these were all English people who were there with me) — then this woman says, "You don't have to be afraid of this, I'll look after it." And just at that time the door opened and the nurse comes in, and then the woman has disappeared, and — everything is as it was in the room except for me.

I was — I felt just as if I had received some infusion of strength or power, and I was not at all anxious any more. And then the nurse says something to the effect that — that now I have to start – she has to help me get dressed because I have to go to Brandon. So I just tell her straight out that I won't go to Brandon. I told her that I am — so I told her that if I needed to go to a hospital, then I would go to Winnipeg, and would go to a physician I knew there.

So she didn't know what to do with me, and went out. Then the physicians came in and they knew — they said this, something to the effect that, how it was that I didn't want to go to Brandon. And I just said that I didn't want to go; I would go to Winnipeg, and that was all.

Then — Ingi had arrived, also, and he said it was quite right that I should go there if I wanted. And then — there were thirty miles to Brandon but there were a hundred and fifty miles to Winnipeg — so they were trying to indicate to me that this would be a terrible journey for me. But it was for naught; I didn't want to hear of anything else.

And then there was ... the railroad — the train left during the latter part of the day, and that's where I went. I was taken there, and I was in a hospital in Winnipeg, had Dr. Brandon, Dr. Olesen, and Dr. McKinnon; they were partners. I had them all. And then they brought innumerable physicians and examined me, and — and they couldn't find any malignancy, but Dr. Brandon said that the kidneys were terrible tired after — after the typhoid fever. And — and they talked a lot about this, and they didn't understand how this — this great physician, there, from Brandon, had found anything – anything that I had to be operated on for. And I was — I was there for about three months, very ill — but I got over it. And, afterwards, I heard that no one had expected I would live, except myself. The physicians, none of the physicians, thought it possible that I would live, in as bad a condition as I was. And what's more, I had a friend who got ill about the same time that I did, from typhoid, and she — and the same thing happened with her kidneys — and she died, but I got over it, to this day.

So when — after I was well enough to be able to travel, then I came here to Arborg and met my foster mother, and I told her this, what had happened to me. I described the woman who had come there, and — and performed these miracles, or whatever one is supposed to call it. And she said I couldn't have described her better, even if I had known her, but I — the description was exactly a description of my mother, who died when I was two years old.

The Haunted House

George H. Ham made a name for himself as a journalist and raconteur; in later years he served as the advertising manager of the Canadian Pacific Railway. In 1877, when he was a thirty-year-old journalist and resident of Winnipeg, he and his wife moved into what he called "the haunted house."

They took possession of a little frame house, just south of old Grace Church on Main Street, Winnipeg. Tradition held that it had been erected on an old Indian burial ground. "During the night queer noises were heard," he wrote in his *Reminiscences of a Raconteur.* "The stove in the adjoining room rattled like mad, and investigation proved nothing. There was no wind or anything else visible that should cause a commotion. A door would slam and on going to it, it was found wide open. One night there was a loud noise as if some tinware hanging up on the wall in the kitchen had fallen ... and so it went on."

The basement was the source of one problem. "One time the cellar was filled with water coming from where, goodness only knows, though it was said that there was a slough through that property years ago. Anyway the cellar was full of water, and it had to be bailed out." Ham procrastinated so his wife engaged some local boys to do the bailing. "But lo and behold, when the trap door was opened, there wasn't a drop of water in the blooming cellar. It was dry as a tin horn.... We never ascertained whence came the water or where it went, but by this time I had got accustomed to the prances and pranks of the house and didn't care a continental."

In due course the Hams moved out and the next tenants found the house not to their liking. "The building was removed to the north end, and some years after, on recognizing it, I called to see if the noises still continued. But they wouldn't let me in."

"I don't pretend to be able to explain the queer noises," Ham concluded. "Whether they were the spirits of the past and gone, Indian braves showing their displeasure at our intrusion in their domain, or were caused by some peculiarity in the construction of the house and its environments, I can not offer an opinion. But, as we got accustomed to them, they didn't disturb us at all, and we got rather proud of our ghostly guests whose board and lodging cost us nothing."

The Haunted Duplex

This story appeared on the Internet. It was posted to a ghost-story newslist to which I subscribe, and I first read it on March 17, 1998. At the time I had no idea of the identity of the author who signed her writing "Lizard," but I wrote to the author and located her in Prince Albert, Saskatchewan. I will let her tell her own story....

Across the street from the fair grounds is a row of older housing authority duplexes. They are all somewhat run down, and the population in the area consists mainly of recently unemployed or unemployable persons. One of these units, on the east side of the second building from the corner, had been re-rented sixteen times in the space of two years, often by people who moved away to identical units in the same row.

A friend of mine was hired to clean this unit and re-do the kitchen floor. He brought along his usual staff of three people, in addition to himself, to do this. When they arrived, things seemed normal enough. All of the surrounding units were empty and waiting to be refurbished in the same manner as this particular one, so it was very quiet. The bathroom upstairs needed some serious help, so my friend went upstairs with the other two men to see to it, while the woman they had brought along to help worked in the kitchen.

While washing the floor, she moved aside the stove and under it was a bloodstain. It looked as fresh and new as if it had just been spilled. She tried to scrub it off, but every time she succeeded, she'd turn her back while the water was drying and it would reappear. After three times doing this, she started to get freaked out and called the men to come down. They all agreed that it was strange, so they ripped up the linoleum. This solved the problem ... for about twenty minutes. Blood started to ooze from the floorboards, looking "half-congealed." She couldn't believe it. She yelled for the men to come down again and they did. They agreed to go home and try again the next day, saying it was probably caused by a dead or dying cat or dog.

The next day, they returned. The bloodstain was on the floorboards, so they decided to re-cover the floor. This took the morning, but when they were done, the floor, one solid piece of linoleum, looked as shiny and new as a show home. Satisfied, they returned to cleaning the upstairs. After about fifteen minutes, the woman in the kitchen dared to look at the floor again. The stain was back, but that wasn't all. That section of the linoleum had somehow reverted to the dingy, grey, dirt encrusted look of the previous lino.

She dropped the bucket she was holding and tried to scrub it clean. Of course, it didn't work. But, as she was scrubbing, the sobbing and screams of a young boy made themselves heard. The men upstairs heard them, too, and came rushing down the stairs. They found the woman had fainted on the kitchen floor, so one of them stayed with her while the others went to find the source of the cries. The sound didn't exist outside, or in the adjoining or surrounding duplexes. Only in that one. They quickly gathered their gear together and left. My friend dropped off his workers at their homes, then went to talk to the people at the housing authority.

It turned out that that unit, which had been built in 1936, had been occupied during the 1960s by a young single mother and her eight-year-old son. They lived relatively quietly, until the boy's father came by one day to see him. The father had an argument with the mother, and a struggle ensued. In the mêlée, the father's gun went off, killing the boy. Both parents ran, not wanting to be charged with murder or manslaughter, leaving the boy to bleed to death alone on the kitchen floor. The linoleum has been changed in the duplex twelve times since that happened, but the blood always came back. None of the tenants who have lived there since have stayed longer than a month, some of them preferring to live on the street than in the unit.

Well, there's the end. My friend only went back once, just to see. The last renovations included two layers of lino. It hadn't helped.

The Ghost Train

It is a matter of record that a head-on collision occurred on July 8, 1908, between the engine for the Spokane *Flyer* and the engine of a passenger train from Lethbridge on the CPR line three kilometres out of Medicine Hat, Alberta. The Lethbridge locomotive was thrown off the tracks and its baggage car was demolished. Seven men were killed, including two engineers, the *Flyer's* Jim Nicholson and the Lethbridge train's Bob Twohey. At the inquest it was established that Nicholson was at fault, having neglected to check that the Lethbridge train had left on time, which it had not.

There were two premonitions of the disaster, and both were witnessed by the railway fireman, Gus Day. The first incident took place two months before the crash. At eleven o'clock one night, Twohey was guiding his engine over the same CPR track three kilometres out of Medicine Hat. Then something astonishing happened. "A huge blinding spotlight suddenly appeared in front of him. He shouted for the fireman, Gus Day, to jump, but it was too late. Twohey fully expected to die. To his amazement, the approaching train veered to the right and flashed past his engine, its whistle blowing. The coach windows were lit and he saw passengers looking out. Now here's the frightening part. *There was only a single rail line running through those hills.*"

That was the first appearance of the Ghost Train. There was no collision — indeed, there was no second train — but the experience so frightened Twohey that he decided to stay off the trains for a while. One month later and on the same stretch of track, the Ghost Train put in its second appearance. Twohey was not at the throttle, having chosen yard work instead, but his friend Nicholson was, and Day was stoking the engine. The same astonishing thing happened. "A dazzling light, a shrieking whistle, and passengers peering out of lighted windows as a train that didn't exist sped past on tracks that didn't exist."

Shortly thereafter the fatal collision occurred. Day was firing up an engine in the yard when he learned of the crash and deaths of his two friends, Nicholson and Twohey. Day pondered the fact that both Nicholson and Twohey had seen the Ghost Train and both were dead. He himself was the only person alive to see both Ghost Trains.

That was the end of the Ghost Trains, at least as far as Day was concerned. He saw them no more. He kept his peace until his retirement in British Columbia in the 1930s. Reading a magazine about a Ghost Train in Colorado, he remembered his experience and recalled it for a reporter. Ted Ferguson told the story in *Sentimental Journey: An Oral History of Train Travel in Canada* (1985).

The Lost Room

Banff Springs Hotel was built overlooking the picturesque beauty of the Bow Valley. The luxury hotel was built by the Canadian Pacific Railway in 1888 in the new resort town of Banff, Alberta. The story goes that in the early 1900s, when the first of the new wings were being added, the architects made a serious error, leaving space for a room with no doors or windows. They revised the blueprints to disguise their error and instructed the builders and workers to seal off the area and keep quiet about it. When the new wing was partly burnt in the fire of 1926, the lost room was found.

It was empty, of course, but attention was drawn to its location along one of the corridors, the very corridor that had been the focus of eerie disturbances. Night watchmen complained that a shadowy figure flitted down this corridor. There were rumours of calls for room service being met by an elderly bellhop, when all the bellhops in the employ of the hotel were young men. No one could figure out who he was.

That is not the end of the strangeness in the hotel. The Rob Roy Lounge is said to have numerous ghostly visitors. Guests have reported seeing the apparition of a bride who falls down the stairway and breaks her neck. Staff members have reported seeing a headless bagpiper, not to mention disembodied carollers in the men's room, as well as a deceased barkeeper who informs imbibers when they have had enough to drink.

The Ghost of Deane House

Deane House is a three-storey, porched house in Calgary that dates back to 1906. It bears the name of Richard Burton Deane, Superintendent of the Royal North-West Mounted Police. Although he disliked the house, he lived in it until 1914, when it was acquired by the Grand Trunk Pacific Railway for use as a railway station and station master's house. It was moved to a new location that year and moved again in 1929. Thereafter it served as a rooming house and an artist's co-op.

Deane House was deserted between 1979 and 1985, and it was then that rumours circulated that it was haunted. From time to time a woman who was said to resemble Deane's wife was seen standing on the enclosed porch. It was said that the murder-suicide of a husband and wife took place during the years it served as a rooming house. There is the suggestion that the house now stands on an old Indian burial ground. Haunted houses burst into flames from time to time. In 1985, there was a fire in the attic and on the third floor, but firemen were fortunately able to bring it under control.

Monika Tremblay, a Calgary psychic, toured the house in 1982 and described her impressions to a television audience as "terrifying."

She said, "As I walked through the front room, it felt like I was walking on Jello, and then I actually witnessed the murder. Right before my eyes, I saw a man chasing a woman with an axe. He then bludgeoned her to death while two children hid in fright in a secret compartment in the kitchen." She also described someone bleeding and stumbling down the steps. In the living room, she saw an old man sitting in a rocking chair, smoking a pipe, and staring out of the window. Her description matched that of Superintendent Deane, the original resident. In the basement, the psychic claimed she encountered an old Indian spirit which said, "This is a secret burial ground — please don't disturb us."

There have been no further reports of spirits or spectres since 1986, when the house was opened to the public as a tea room and history museum.

Capitol Hill House

A nondescript bungalow located in the Capitol Hill district of Calgary was the scene of a bizarre disappearance in March 1929. According to writer and researcher W. Ritchie Benedict, a reclusive man named Thomas C. Hall vanished. Nineteen years later his remains were found below the floorboards of the house, semi-mummified in the soil. He had been shot in the head. Although the police identified a suspect — a friend of the recluse who had often played cards with him — there was no proof that he was the murderer.

That should have been the end of it, but it was not. The body was found in 1948. Cecil Pearce, the owner of the house from 1948 to 1956, reported that before the discovery of the corpse his three daughters had complained that "a mysterious clammy hand" had poked one of them. Also prior to the discovery was the experience of a previous owner, Elizabeth Irish, who often admitted to feeling uneasy in the house. As late as August 1982, Rick Passey, a young steelworker who lived there, grumbled about unexplained knockings at the front door.

Edith Taylor, who had lived in the neighbourhood for forty years, always felt that there was something unnatural about the house. She recalled that not long after the discovery of the body, a horrible thing had happened. The families that lived in the three houses which were set in the shape of a triangle on land once used by Hall to graze his horses — he was a teamster — all reported the deaths of children. She said Hall's house had been a source of bad luck to everyone who has lived there. Families were always breaking up. In one instance, a husband chased his wife around the block with a knife.

Canmore Opera House Ghost

The Canmore Opera House was built in the late nineteenth century for the use of the miners of Canmore, Alberta. Then it was used as a hospital and retirement home until 1960, when it was abandoned. Five years later the building was moved to Calgary where it is now part of the city's Heritage Park.

In its new location the Opera House was put to good use by musical and dramatic groups until 1985. It was during the summer of 1975 that performers and employees alike began to note that a number of odd things were happening. The administrative director of Alberta Theatre Projects was quoted as saying, "I'm reluctant to state we have a ghost, but a large number of staff people claim to have either seen or heard what they say is a ghost." She herself saw nothing but added, "I've had a feeling there was something present and heard someone walking upstairs in the building when there was definitely no one else around. It's not a publicity stunt either! There have been a lot of incidents that we haven't been able to explain."

Many of the inexplicable incidents centre around a man with long blond hair who is dressed in turn-of-the-century clothing. A historian employed by Heritage Park noted that the man in question, who seems to enjoy eavesdropping on the theatrical productions, fits the description of Sam Livingston, a homesteader on the original grounds of Heritage Park who died in 1897. Since he was an Irishman, the suggestion is that his spirit enjoys listening to musicals now and then.

Two directors of the Alberta Psychic Society spent a night at the Opera House during the winter of 1974-75. The next morning they claimed that they felt "some kind of presence there." They determined that the presence was persistent but not malevolent.

The last known report of anyone sensing anything was in the early 1980s, when during a theatrical performance, two actresses complained to the stage manager about a stranger who had been allowed backstage. They said they saw a man sitting on the stairs. When the stage manager checked, there was no trace of anyone.

It is difficult to know whether or not such manifestations will continue since the Opera House is no longer a venue for theatrical presentations. If the managers of Heritage Park decide to shut down the Opera House, then (to paraphrase writer Shirley Jackson), "What ever walks there will walk alone."

Ghosts of Banff and Lake Louise

Tourists travel around the world to see the magnificent scenery of the Rocky Mountains at Banff and Lake Louise. Skiers come to ski the slopes, not to see the ghosts.

Wayne MacDonald had ghosts in mind. A reporter for the *Calgary Albertan,* he wrote an account of a night he spent in Halfway House in Banff National Park and published it in that newspaper on February 3, 1962. The account was so popular that he wrote a second account of an experience at Lake Louise that was published two days later.

There is more on those slopes than snow!

Halfway House, Banff National Park – Dozens of skiers have fled from this country ski lodge late at night.

They believe it is haunted. I wanted to run on the first night of my visit here to check their stories. Not that I believe in ghost stories, but strange things happen in Halfway.

Frightening things happen, especially at night, but despite my imagination, they can all be explained — so far — by using common sense.

That's the hardest thing up here — common sense.

I skied into Halfway with guide-companion Glenn Cowan late Wednesday afternoon. The cabin itself is one-roomed, log, and situated high on a knoll in a wind-swept valley. Immediately to the east the blank cliffs of Redoubt Mountain tower high in the frosty air.

To the south, Mt. Temple reaches for the gods and beyond that the Valley of the Ten Peaks nestles on the horizon.

The cabin has two bunk beds, a steel one and a wooden one. It has two stoves, one of which doesn't work.

There's a wooden table, a wooden bench, a wash stand, some cookware and plates, and that's all.

Glenn and I arrived in time for supper. After bacon, eggs and fried bread, he left.

The sun was lowering behind the peaks as he started; the evening was still.

My mind was working overtime. I heard new noises — creaks and groans. The crackling fire startled me, and I imagined a broom in the corner had moved.

I told myself that ghosts don't exist.

As night came on, it worried me that the sky was black. There were no stars; the moon was hidden.

A wind was starting to wheeze in the pines and even this sound was unfriendly.

I tried to read. I placed three candles on the table and huddled close to the book. Each new sound jerked me from the pages. I found myself stepping to the window, fighting the reflection of the candles in the glass, peering into the blackness.

I finally admitted that no matter what, I was in Halfway for the night. I could never find the trail to Temple chalet without moonlight.

I returned to my reading. Suddenly, without warning, two candles blew out.

I lit them again and sat, almost fearing to move. When I did I found an eight-inch crack in the log by the window. The wind had extinguished the candles.

I decided, shortly after 7:00 p.m., that the best place would be bed. The fire was burning low; I had been warned not to burn too many candles. I felt sleep would drown my fears.

In bed the noises magnified. I heard a low creaking and something banging on the door, but I had been warned of this. The wind often rocks an overhead sign on the cabin.

The fire was now dead, save for final glowing embers. I fell asleep. An hour later, I awakened in terror. Bright shadows were leaping across the room. My immediate reaction was that the moon had risen. But this light was too bright.

I silently reached for my glasses. The fire was raging.

A full, orange blaze was crackling in the stove, hot and bright and loud. I was terrified.

After ageless minutes I rationalized. There must have been an unburned log in the stove. It must have caught fire after I fell asleep.

The night went without further event. I wakened in the morning to a cry of "anybody home?" A park warden stepped in, tripping on the bench I had placed against the door. He was on his way to Skoki and stopped to check how I was.

How was I?

Oh, Halfway's fine — in daylight.

———

Lake Louise — A grey-haired man turned to me in the coffee shop of the Post Hotel. "So you spent two nights in Halfway House?" he asked.

I replied I had.

"Son," he said, "you're mighty lucky to be alive."

The man was Ray LeGace, manager of the hotel and a twenty-year veteran of the Rockies. He's like most residents of Lake Louise; he honestly believes there are ghosts in Halfway House.

"I'd never stay there alone," he said. "In fact, I don't think I'd stay there at all. Especially at night."

Ray believes the tiny skiers' cabin halfway between Lake Louise and Skoki Lodge is occupied by the ghost of a Calgary painter who died there several years ago.

The painter and his dog lived in Halfway for several months. He refused to come out in even the bitterest weather because he was waiting for a perfect mountain sunset.

He wanted to see a "perfect" sun dip behind Redoubt Mountain – but it never happened. The painter was never satisfied with the colours of the sky.

He starved to death in the lonely lodge.

Others in Lake Louise believe the ghost to be a woman, an attractive girl killed in an avalanche. Or two brothers buried in snow in the 1930s. Or a mountain-born skier killed on Mount Ptarmigan.

Everyone you talk to has a different tale to tell. Only a handful will say there's no ghost.

My second night in Halfway was much like the first. An over-imaginative mind was my greatest foe.

I had busied myself during the day, melting snow, washing dishes, writing, preparing food. There were no fears in daylight, but as darkness fell, uneasiness returned.

The loneliness was hardest; the knowledge that no matter what, I couldn't get out. I had never skied before my journey in, and I could never find my way to Temple Chalet without a guide.

The darkness on the second night brought with it a storm. It snowed heavily, and the wind came up, whistling through the pines, pounding on the lodge, banging at the windows, sniffing at the candles.

But at the same time, it was melting.

Water dripped throughout the night from the roof, splatting on the snow around the cabin. The dripping sounded — in my mind — like footsteps in the snow.

Drip, drip, drip. Step, step, step.

Was someone out there?

I buried my head in my pillow and tried to sleep.

The wind again banged the sign above the cabin door. It crashed against the logs, fell back, crashed, fell back, crashed.

The sign is suspended from three links of chain. The chain, when the sign wasn't banging, grated against the metal hook, creaking and groaning. It was a horrible sound.

And the crackling of the fire bothered me. I started every time a chunk of wood "popped" in the heat. It would seem the fire was finally dead, and suddenly, "Crack."

But the ghost — or ghosts — didn't come.

I wakened in the morning to a voice — a distant yodel. By the time I dressed, Glenn Cowan was at the door to guide me back to Temple.

He seemed partly disappointed, partly relieved, that the ghost who visited him hadn't visited me. When he stayed at Halfway a fortnight ago, he was startled when his fire suddenly went out. He turned to see a plate on the middle of the table move to the edge and crash to the floor. A cup in its saucer on the table tipped.

As he hurried to get his skies on to escape the "thing," he suddenly smelled a woman's perfume. "It was as if I was helping a woman on with her coat," he said, "and I suddenly smelled the perfume in her hair."

Is there a ghost in Halfway? A ghost that has haunted Cowan and skiers by the score? A ghost that keeps Ray LeGace away?

I don't know.

The people who have fled Halfway cannot be swayed. They're convinced the ghost is there.

On the other hand, skiers have stayed in the cabin for weeks, for months, and more. One stayed throughout a winter.

I doubt the ghost is there — but can I say? A prime minister of Canada believed in them, and writers have told of them through the years.

We scoff at their beliefs, but who can tell?

WEST COAST

The Ghost Photograph

Visitors to the Provincial Archives of the Parliament Buildings in Victoria often pause in front of one of the vintage photographs on permanent display. This is the celebrated Ghost Photograph.

The photograph is an eye-catcher. It is a group photograph that shows a row of gentlemen standing outdoors in the snow in front of the Colonial Government Buildings at New Westminster. There are eleven gentlemen in all, or is it twelve? One of the figures looks insubstantial, ghost-like, and therein lies a story.

The photograph shows all eleven members of the first Legislative Council at New Westminster, plus the clerk. The clerk, a gentleman named Charles Good, swore that he was unavoidably absent on the day the photograph was taken. Yet there is his image, second from the right. The gentlemen are (from left to right): Henry Holbrook, George A. Walkem, W.O. Hamley, Charles Brew, H.M. Ball, A.N. Birch, C.W. Franks, Peter O'Reilly, Walter Moberly, J.A.R. Homer, Charles Good, H.P.P. Crease. An examination of Good's image reveals it to be unique in that unlike the others it is slightly blurry and somewhat transparent.

Not much is remembered of Charles Good. He was born in Dorset, England, attended Oxford, and shortly afterwards settled on the West Coast. He was appointed chief clerk in the Office of the Colonial Secretary in 1859. When the Legislative Council was established, Good became its clerk and held that appointment until 1867 when he was promoted to the position of Assistant Colonial Secretary. He became Acting Colonial Secretary and, following Confederation, Assistant (later Deputy) Provincial Secretary and Clerk to the Legislative Assembly. He retired to Devon. The date of his death is unknown. One would judge him to be a responsible person and an important colonial official in 1865 when the photographic portrait was taken. Today his life and career are forgotten by all but West Coast historians; only his hazy image in the so-called Ghost Photograph brings him to mind.

The group photograph was scheduled to be taken on January 13, 1865. But the date was delayed out of deference to the state of Good's health. He was unwell; indeed, the rumour had circulated that he had died. The taking of the photograph was delayed eight days, until January 21. Good was still confined to his sickbed and unable to be there "in person." Nevertheless the councillors posed without their clerk. The picture was snapped and developed. When Good recovered, he was shown the print and no one was more surprised than Charles Good to see his own face in it.

After more than a century and a quarter it is impossible to establish for a fact the whereabouts of Good on the day of the sitting, whenever that was, for even that is in some doubt. Yet an examination of the *Journals* of the Legislative Council suggests that Good was in attendance and discharging his official duties as clerk throughout the month of January. Therefore, he was in good health and not at all ill. He was probably in attendance for the sitting. Why then is his image so ghost-like? It appears somewhat blurry and transparent, and the apparent reason for this is that Good's image is "underexposed." He was a busy man and he was late for the sitting. He slipped into place later than the rest of the gentlemen, taking his place somewhat behind them. Photographic plates were slow in those days, and the photographer had to take a long "time" exposure. It was, perhaps, a "time" exposure and Good was not "on time."

No doubt Good, whether on his sickbed or not, chuckled over the photograph when a print was presented to him. The practical man that he was, he would have chuckled all the harder, had he known that visitors to the Provincial Archives of the Parliament Buildings in Victoria would be marvelling at his ghostly image more than a century and a quarter later!

The Headless Brakeman

There is a Headless Brakeman who is said to haunt the CPR yards at the foot of Granville Street in Vancouver. Reports of his presence there have been made by railway employees since 1928.

That was the year Hub Clark, a railway brakeman, lost his head in the yards. One dark and rainy night, he slipped and fell off a freight train and his head hit the rails next to the freight track. He was knocked unconscious and a passenger train, speeding down the track, severed his head from his body, two inches below his Adam's apple.

Thereafter stories circulated about how a headless man in railway overalls was seen in the yard on dark and rainy nights. Apparently for years Vancouver railwaymen joked, "Don't throw your pumpkin away after Halloween. Hub Clark can use it."

The apparition was last sighted by a railway worker on a dark and rainy night in 1942. The Headless Brakeman was darting between boxcars in search of his head.

The Chilliwack Poltergeist

Weird disturbances of a poltergeist character were noted in Chilliwack, British Columbia, during the winter of 1951-52. They occurred in the four-room cottage owned and occupied by Anna Duryba, a Ukrainian woman. The disturbances commenced shortly after Miss Duryba invited into her home her fourteen-year-old niece, Kathleen.

A.J. Edwards, an employee in the local sheriff's office, was sent to investigate neighbours' reports of loud and violent hammerings on the walls, accompanied by occasional flights of objects that caused damage to the windows. After examining the matter, Edwards came to the conclusion that "some person" was intent on having Miss Duryba leave the house. This was also the opinion of Miss Duryba's brother, Alex, who lived close by. Alex "took down his shotgun and stationed himself at the basement window of his sister's house, prepared to frighten away the intruder. From his post he shot off a series of bullets, accompanied with threats addressed to the ghost — but without the slightest effect."

Psychical researcher R.S. Lambert in his book *Exploring the Supernatural in Canada* (1955) made the following point about the rest of the affair:

In fact, the knockings grew worse. They occurred as often as thirty times in one night, and were heard by persons standing within six feet of the spot. Once they were heard when the house was floodlit and surrounded by a posse of neighbours. Sometimes they even occurred during daylight.

The Mayor of Chilliwack, Mr. T.T. McCammon, who had known Miss Duryba for many years, and vouched for her excellent character, felt sure she had no enemies or any other personal connexion with the occurrences. Who then could be the person referred to by Mr. Edwards as wishing to drive her from her home?

Certainly Miss Duryba did not want to go — in fact, she flatly refused to evacuate the haunted premises. But at the suggestion of the Rev. W.T. Clarke, Mr. Edwards arranged that her niece, Kathleen, who was far from robust and suffered from "nerves," should be sent away for an extended holiday. Kathleen stayed for ten days in Vancouver, and during her absence the manifestations completely ceased. Then soon after her return to Chilliwack they began again!

Many observers would have liked to pursue the matter further, and trace the connexion that appeared to exist between the niece and the noises. But Miss Anna Duryba and her brother, Alex, had formed quite other theories about the disturbances. In their opinion, the whole affair was the product of "racial prejudice" on the part of some of her neighbours. For this reason, they strongly deprecated any more investigations and refused to co-operate in them. So a veil of silence descended over the Duryba household, bringing a sudden and disappointing end to the history of this intriguing Chilliwack poltergeist.

———

Lambert went on to quote the detailed report made by Edwards of the sheriff's office:

———

I am unable to explain the means used to cause the poundings on the outer walls of the home. I have determined beyond doubt that the sounds are not caused by electrical mechanisms in the house, nor are they connected with a nearby radio transmitter or aircraft radio beams. Animals, birds and sub-surface earth movements have also been ruled out.

I have heard the sounds on four occasions. In each case they have come as rapid, violent rappings on the outer wall near a window. All persons in the house were within my range of vision on these occasions, with the exception of Miss Duryba's teen-age niece, who was asleep in her bedroom. Each time I ran outside, but could see no one, although the house was fully floodlit.

The sounds usually lasted between one and two minutes, and

sounded almost as though they might be made with a pneumatic hammering device. The second time, I was outside making an inspection at the time the sounds were heard. I was thus able to observe the source of the sounds at close range. Absolutely nothing could be seen. I determined that no person inside the house was responsible, and later checked to see if anything was in the wall.

On the four occasions when I heard the sounds, they came between 8:00 p.m. and midnight. I am told they have been heard regularly during the day, as well as at night. Windows have been broken on several occasions, including one kitchen window which was broken after it had been protected by a wire screen and sheet of plastic.

After considering all factors and making thorough investigations, I have reason to believe some person is trying to drive Miss Duryba from her home.

The Spirit of the Hanging Judge

Here is a ghost story that is rich in the history of the West Coast.

Sir Matthew Baillie Begbie was an Old Country barrister who was appointed chief justice of the mainland of British Columbia in 1866. He was nicknamed the Hanging Judge for his fair but summary decisions.

Is the spirit of the Hanging Judge still hanging around? Jean Kozocari believed that in some sense Sir Matthew's spirit remained on the earthly plane for at least three-quarters of a century following his death in 1894. Kozocari, a native of Victoria, was a practitioner of wicca. In the company of two mediums, she visited a bungalow built in the 1950s in Saanich, north of Victoria, that its present occupants believed to be haunted or at least to be the focus of poltergeist activity. Previous occupants had a long list of complaints about the place – swarms of flies, a plague of rats, strange noises, and peculiar movements. They said they felt that the bungalow was in some sense "unliveable." Kozocari and the mediums immediately felt that something was awry.

Kozocari's first visit took place on Father's Day 1980. Over the next three years she made repeat visits to the house until it was acquired by new owners. During her visits she noted the nature of the disturbances. Whatever was affecting the house was resistant to the rite of exorcism. Dowsers came up with nothing. At one point the letter

M was found scratched into the silver of a large mirror firmly mounted on a bedroom wall.

Kozocari sensed that the disturbances emanated from the basement of the house, which rested on solid rock. The rock oozed an oily, aluminum-coloured substance. There seemed to be no rhyme or reason to the disturbances. In researching the history of the property, she learned that the land had once been owned by Sir Matthew Baillie Begbie. In those days it was simply a tract of land without any dwellings. Apparently Sir Matthew was quite attached to his property, and from time to time he would ride out to visit it, sitting for hours on the large rock and staring out into space.

Kozocari took a number of photographs of the bungalow. They were clear except where the building rested on the rock. Here all detail was lost behind a peculiar pillar of white that appeared on the photograph. One final photographic negative, taken of the house as a whole, was found to depict a curly-haired, white-bearded man sporting a cowboy-like hat, the very image of the older Sir Matthew.

Did the *M* in the mirror stand for Matthew? Kozocari believed that it did, and that his spirit was responsible for the disturbances, for whatever reason. "His very strong presence made it possible for other and later things to manifest," she added.

The house now has new owners and occupants who may or may not have noted the disturbances.

Pursuit by Lightning

There are people who are blessed, and some people who are cursed. One person who suffered the latter fate was Major Sumerford. He was cursed by bolts of lightning.

The following account of the accident-prone life of Major Sumerford is based on Albert A. Brandt's article "Lightning to the End," published in *Fate* in April-May 1952.

Probably no man was ever more relentlessly pursued by lightning than Major R. Sumerford, late of Vancouver, British Columbia. Fate first struck in 1918, in Flanders, while the Major was on patrol. He was hit by a bolt that killed his horse and left him paralyzed from the waist down. An invalid, he returned to his home in Vancouver, and eventually recovered enough to walk with the aid of two canes.

In 1924, the Major and three friends went on a fishing trip to a mountain lake. His friends left to get some supplies, leaving the major sitting under a tree. A sudden storm blew up. Lightning struck the tree, and his friends returned to find that he had been struck and that the right side of his body was paralyzed. He was removed to a hospital, and it required more than two years for him to recover.

One day during the summer of 1930, Major Sumerford was walking with friends in a Vancouver park. Again there was a sudden storm. The group hurried toward the canopy of a refreshment stand, but before the major could reach shelter, he was felled by a bolt of lightning. This time he was permanently paralyzed and confined to a wheelchair until he died two years later.

But even death did not stop the grim pursuit. On a July night in 1934, a violent electrical storm raged over Vancouver. A bolt of lightning struck the cemetery, completely destroying a single tombstone. The shattered stone had marked the grave of former British cavalry officer, Major Sumerford.

The Oak Bay Hauntings

The district of Oak Bay, with its exclusive Victoria Golf Course, overlooks the Strait of Georgia. It seems that the property has a host of ghosts that also overlook the Strait....

The rambling frame house on Heron Street in Oak Bay was built in 1851 by John Tod upon his retirement as chief trader for the Hudson's Bay Company in what is now Western Canada. Successive owners of the house have complained to the press of a series of strange happenings. Writing in 1950, a journalist noted that "doors open themselves, windows crawl up the frames, and a rocking chair sometimes rocks when no human form occupies it. Several times all the hats have dropped from the rack in the front hall when there was no wind or vibration to explain it."

During World War II, two Royal Canadian Air Force pilots spent one night, and one night only, in the house. They declared

they were awakened at night by the rattling of chains. They "saw in the corner an Indian woman fettered hand and foot. The figure then disappeared after an appealing gesture."

Mrs. E.C. Turner, a subsequent occupant, vowed that she was moving out right away and would never return to the house. "She often awoke at night to see her bedroom door swinging slowly open.... At night her cat would snarl and spit for no obvious reason."

Renovating the house and grounds in 1951, workmen digging in the garden unearthed a skeleton that had been buried seven feet deep. It was at least a century old. It was noted at the time that "the broad acres of the Tod estate were once the scene of a great battle of rival Indians. Many died in battle and were buried where they fell."

Indeed, the area seems to attract a hoard of ghosts. Another journalist exclaimed, "A whole community of ghosts may be seen on the rock-strewn beach and, if the sea is quiet, their chorus of lamentations will be audible."

In April 1964, a student named Anthony Gregson was strolling with a friend across the greens when they witnessed the ghostly gathering:

It was a little after 9:00 p.m. and we were walking on the golf course. My friend had been out here on other occasions and was telling me once she saw the whole community of ghosts on the beach, even heard them. We joked about ghosts for a while and suddenly we became very serious. We didn't see anything, but we could feel a definite change in the atmosphere.

Then we saw the ghost. She was about 1,000 yards away and appeared to be running over the stones on the beach without touching them. I assumed it was the ghost of a woman because it appeared to have a dress on. She was a luminous grey with an aura about her. When she reached the furthermost point of land she stopped and looked into the sea as if she were expecting someone. I would rather like to think she was.

We must have watched her for five minutes and my friend assured me I wasn't seeing things. The ghost moved with much more ease than a human and had a certain grace of action, especially in her arms. Other features were less distinct.

There is no doubt ... now. I am certain of what I saw. I returned to the golf course the next day and checked all land formations to make sure I was not mistaken. I believe in leaving ghosts to their own lives. I am not going back there again. It was an unnerving experience.

Perhaps the pale figure that Gregson saw was the ghost of Doris Gravelin, whose strangled body was buried in a sand trap here in the mid-1930s. Victor Gravelin, her estranged husband, was the prime suspect, but before he could be charged with his young wife's murder, he drowned himself in the waters here.

Doris's ghost has made annual appearances since 1936, usually in late March, sometimes in early April. She is known as the April Ghost. According to the late Robin Skelton, poet and witch, "Between 4:30 and 5:00 p.m., she has been seen walking across the golf course, looking entirely normal, though slightly old fashioned. It is only when she has passed by that the watcher feels anything unusual and experiences a kind of dread as she turns and looks back over her shoulder. Later, between 9:30 and 10 in the evening, she appears on the golf course close to the water. She stands with her arms outstretched, wearing a long white dress. She rushes towards you then suddenly shrinks into a small pool of light and disappears. In this particular guise she appears only to courting or engaged couples, and never to married persons." Skelton suggested that her presence seems to be a warning to courting couples of the dangers of marriage. "The ghost of Doris has been seen and felt by a great many people over the years," he added.

The Case of the Snoring Ghost

Margery Wighton, a Vancouver-based journalist, is the contributor of this account of a haunting. It was published under the title "The Case of the Haunted House and Snoring Ghost" in the *Vancouver Sun* on December 27, 1952. No doubt the editors decided that a "snoring ghost" made delightful reading between Christmas and New Year's, Marley's ghost and all that!

In the 1960s, whenever anyone reported "mystery lights," it was commonplace to suggest that the cause was "swamp gas." Nowadays, whenever a house in Canada is haunted, someone suggests that it was erected on an old Indian burial ground.

It was the early summer of 1912. I was fifteen and living in British Columbia with my parents.

Quite unexpectedly, my father had a very good offer for our fruit farm in the Okanagan Valley, and we moved to Vancouver Island where he intended to start a poultry farm. We bought twelve acres of uncleared bush and arranged for the delivery of a sectional bungalow.

The problem was to find somewhere to live for about eight weeks while the bungalow was under construction. This matter was soon solved by the offer of a shack, belonging to a farmer, standing on the other side of a deep ravine, amid giant fir trees and thick undergrowth.

For the first few days, things were normal enough, and tired with helping my father unravel the plans of our bungalow, we came home each evening, and after supper were only too pleased to go to bed.

The third night, I went upstairs about nine o'clock and, while undressing, my mother sat on my bed talking to me. We had left my father reading in the little sitting-room. In the middle of her conversation, my mother stopped abruptly and laughed. My father was snoring downstairs!

"Daddy must be tired," she said. We both listened to a comfortable, monotonous snore, so distinct one would have imagined the sleeper to be in the room.

My mother rose and walked downstairs and I followed in my dressing gown. "I thought you were asleep," she said. "We heard you snoring."

My father was indignant. "You must both be mad," he said. "I'm reading a good book."

We came upstairs again, and no sooner had I taken off my dressing gown than we realized the snore was continuing. "Really," my mother said, "Daddy must be teasing us."

We laughed to relieve the tension, took off our shoes, and crept downstairs again, thinking to find my father pretending to snore. To our astonishment, we found him, as before, busy reading.

He looked annoyed and took off his glasses. "If you two think this is awfully amusing, I don't," he said.

The laughter died from our lips. We told him about the snoring. He said we were still crazy and reluctantly followed us upstairs. And there it was again! Just a quiet, peaceful human snore.

"There's someone in here," my father exclaimed, getting up impatiently. "But where?" he asked, looking around the bare walls, where there wasn't even a cupboard.

We banged about, thumping the walls, hitting the wooden ceiling. We moved the bed and table around but the snoring continued. We ransacked the second bedroom, but as we passed through the doorway we could not hear it any more.

My father went to the little kitchen, at the foot of the stairs, while my mother and I stood at the top. We said "there" each time the snore came. He could not hear anything downstairs at all.

We then decided it must be something outside. But as we stood together outside the little shack, there was not a sound to be heard but the far away cry of a night bird in the bush.

My father then stood under my low bedroom window, while my mother and I went back to my room. The snoring went on unabated but my father could hear nothing whatever.

Completely nonplussed, my mother and I went to bed in the second bedroom. My father determined not to sleep till he had "laid the ghost."

The moon shone through the windows and I found myself unable to sleep. At 2:00 a.m., my father came into the room. "I'm damned if I can stand it," he said. "I've tried everything to stop that snore. I thought I'd found one of you two snoring now."

Next day he and the owner raked the roof from end to end. That was really all they could do, since there was no loft and the place had no foundations. We could see under the flooring boards and there was absolutely nothing.

When evening came, the owner returned to see if he could hear the snoring, and sure enough it started again most punctually. Night after night our "snorer" enjoyed his slumbers while we had little rest.

People suggested owls, deer, chipmunks, spiders, and Indian tom-toms. But outside suggestions were disposed of, since once you left my bedroom you could hear nothing.

My father couldn't stand it and slept downstairs, while mother and I nervously occupied the second bedroom.

And we stood this for six weeks, with no hope of solving the mystery. Then our architect friend, Clem Webb, arrived. We told him all about our snoring ghost.

We congregated in the little bedroom once more, as we had done so often. Nine o'clock came, nine-thirty, ten. Nothing happened, for the first time for six weeks!

Clem Webb never heard it. He completely laid the ghost, and we never heard it again. We moved into our own bungalow about three weeks after his arrival, and almost forgot all about it.

But a year later, the owner of the shack wrote to a Vancouver firm for a new car. When it arrived, driven by a man from the garage, he decided he must have a few lessons before allowing the man to return to Vancouver. Having no room for him in the house, he put the driver to sleep in the haunted shack.

At midnight there was a wild knocking on his door and there stood the driver, trembling from head to foot.

"The place is haunted," the man kept repeating. "I heard someone come in, although I locked the door, walk upstairs and throw his boots off. Then the next thing I knew he was snoring loudly. Yet there's not a soul there, I went all round with a lamp."

He refused to return and left next morning.

The shack was still standing in its lonely setting among the tall dark pines when I visited the place in 1937. It was empty and had been for some years, people said.

I wandered once more through the deep gully, along the trail over the dried pine needles. The maple leaves had turned a burnished gold, and no one standing in that quiet spot would ever dream that such a disturbing mystery haunted the little shack.

Perhaps the Indians are nearest the truth. They say it's built over an old Indian burial ground.

Who knows?

See the Dancing Indians

Jack Scott was a respected newspaperman whose byline delighted generations of Vancouver readers. "The Night I Began to Believe in Ghosts" is the title of Scott's reminiscence about the dream or vision he had of "dancing Indians."

Last weekend marked the tenth anniversary of my belief in ghosts, after a lifetime of scoffing at the supernatural and pshawing at the psychic, and it was fitting or coincidental or something that once more we were camped on the Valdez spit.

Let us now do a fast dissolve to that summer's day a decade ago when we packed our little sloop with a week's provisions and set off to meander down the water corridors of the Gulf Islands.

We had just the one commitment, a rendezvous with Gordon Graham, a longtime friend of mine who was then the entire RCMP detachment at Ganges on Saltspring Island, and his attractive wife, Lou. The plan was to meet us at the inside entrance to Porlier Pass, which separates Galiano and Valdez islands and where the fishing at this time of year is superb.

"We may not get there until around sunset," Gordon had said, "so it might be a good idea to set up camp before we arrive. There are some spots north of the spit on Valdez Island with a good shelter for the boats and close enough to the Pass so that we can get fishing at first light. We'll look for you there next Friday night. Leave a couple of coho for us."

My wife and I had a sinfully pleasant week cruising through the islands, timing it so that we arrived at Porlier on the Friday. We took our limit of blueback along the kelp line outside the full boil of the Pass and then went through at slack water and along the eastern shoreline of Valdez until I found the anchorage Gordon had mentioned.

It was a pleasant campsite. There is a sharply sloping beach of clamshell sun-bleached so white that it gleams like marble in the moonlight. We'd rigged a heavy tarpaulin as a tent on a grassy ledge behind the line of driftwood. At our back the cliff rose steeply into heavy timbers.

When the Grahams arrived at dusk in their little speedboat we pan-fried two of the blueback, watching the sun set over Vancouver Island and wondering what the poor people might be doing.

We sat a long time by the fire that night, watching the moon rising over Galiano and throwing its light on the still dark water of Trincamali Channel, and it was around midnight when we built up the fire with heavy slabs of bark, said goodnight, and crawled into our sleeping bags.

It must have been around two or three in the morning when I was awakened by the sound of tom-toms. I lay in the bedroll, looking up at the reflection of the dying fire on the canvas overhead and wondering why I felt no alarm.

"It must be a dream," I thought, but then I knew it was not and I raised myself on one elbow and turned my eyes to the fire.

Beyond the glowing embers I could see a great crowd of Indians dancing in the moonlight. They appeared to be in full ceremonial dress. There was no sound from them, only the steady, muffled rhythm of the drums as they moved gracefully and sinuously in and out of the perimeter of the beach fire.

It was a beautiful sight to see, so much so that I felt no apprehension whatever, merely a delight.

I watched them for several minutes and then I leaned over to my wife to awaken her. "Come and see the dancing Indians," I was going to say.

At that moment Graham rolled over in his bedroll, got up noisily and threw several great pieces of bark on the fire. The tom-toms stopped. The Indians faded away. There was only the slope of the clamshell beach, white in the moonbeams.

I lay back in the sleeping bag, marvelling at what I'd heard and seen and the next thing I knew it was dawn.

I did not mention the experience the next morning, perhaps because my wife is subject to extravagant dreams and I am generally so ill-tempered at her recounting them in great detail that I felt it wiser to keep this experience to myself.

I say experience rather than dream because the reality of it was so vivid that I walked along the beach looking for moccasin prints. There was, of course, nothing. No more than fifteen minutes later I had hooked into a thirty-two-pound spring salmon and that had the further effect of pushing the incident from my mind.

A week later Graham phoned me and suggested I drop down to the RCMP office to see something interesting.

On his desk was the mummified body of a young person and two sun-bleached skulls, also children's. They had been found on Valdez Island earlier in the week by two exploring boys.

"I've just been talking to a man in Victoria who's an expert on these things," Graham said. "He tells me they're from the burying grounds of the Haida Indians.

"And you know where they were found? Right where we had our camp that night! Seems there's a thousand or more Haidas buried all along the beach there, many of them victims of a plague of smallpox. "Boy, I'll bet you'd have had a restless night if you'd known you were sleeping on top of these things."

I had then told Graham the story, just as I've told it above, as it happened, and Gordon, owning that he, himself, had felt some strange presence that night, suggested that one day we must return and hold a vigil, a suggestion he made only half in jest.

That was exactly ten years ago and it wasn't until this last weekend that I found myself able to return to the island.

On Friday night and on Saturday night we were camped in exactly the same place on the Valdez spit with two other friends. None of us heard tom-toms. None of us saw a single dancing figure in the glow of the beach fire. Indeed, it was all so ordinary that I couldn't resist phoning my old friend who is now up the Island.

"I guess it was a dream after all," I said.

"Now, just a minute," Gordon said. "What was the weather like Friday and Saturday night?"

"Pouring," I said. "We were drenched both nights."

"Well, I forgot to tell you what that expert told me in Victoria," Graham said. "The Indian ghosts only dance in the moonlight."

A Lady in the House

There is a small house in a quiet suburb of Vancouver that is haunted by the spirit of its former owner. The spirit appeared on only one occasion and it seemed pleased with what it saw. It has not been in evidence since 1972.

I am grateful to Sylvia Taylor for sharing this experience with my readers and me. Mrs. Taylor, like her husband, was born and educated in England. Both hold degrees in the biological sciences. They came to Canada in 1968 and settled in Vancouver. The account comes from letters that she sent to me on June 4 and July 15, 1987.

My husband and I bought a small house in Vancouver in early 1972. The two-bedroom house is located in a middle-class neighbourhood in the southern part of the city, about half a mile north of the Fraser River. The assessor could not find any information on the exact date that the house was built, but he estimated that 1943-45 was the probable period of its construction, as these were the years that services were laid onto the site. Therefore the house was about twenty-eight years old when we bought it. At the time we were in our early thirties and had no children.

Some weeks after moving into the house in March, my husband and I were sitting around the dining-room table enjoying dinner and chatting merrily. I was seated with my back to the window at the front of the house, facing a door that led into a small squarish hallway from which opened two more doors. The door directly opposite the dining-room door led to the bathroom, while the other door opened to the left into the kitchen. The kitchen and dining-room doors were open, and my husband was sitting with his left shoulder towards the hallway, facing the side of the house.

I suddenly stopped talking, as I saw a woman walk through the dining-room doorway and stop about two feet away from my husband. My face apparently changed in appearance, as my husband turned to his left to see what I was staring at. The woman had disappeared. He did not see her. He is skeptical when it comes to ghosts, but he is convinced that I did see something.

The whole incident lasted only a few seconds, but the woman appeared to me with perfect clarity. She was an elderly person, in her late fifties or early sixties, with a pleasant face and dark grey hair seemingly drawn back into a bun or similar hairstyle. She was wearing a high-necked, long-sleeved, light-coloured blouse and a skirt of dark, heavy material. I got the impression that the skirt was longish (falling well below her knees) and that she was wearing heavy stockings and sensible shoes. In other words, she was somewhat old-fashioned in dress.

Over the blouse and skirt was a flowered apron with a bib top and straps over the shoulders. She had one corner of the apron skirt in her hands as if wiping them. Her attitude was one of coming to see that guests were comfortable and satisfied. I could almost hear her say, before she disappeared, "Is everything all right? Good!"

The incident was in no way scary. In fact, it was rather the opposite, as though we had been checked by a caring hostess and as if she herself was satisfied with what she saw.

The previous owners of the house were a childless couple, a few years older than ourselves, who had moved into a larger, more expensive place. The realtor had told us that they had owned the house for about six years. After the appearance of the lady, we asked some gentle questions of the neighbours (without telling them the reason for our curiosity) about previous occupants.

Their information was that the childless couple had lived in the house for no more than three years. The owners before them had been two middle-aged ladies. One or both of them were schoolteachers, and one of them had committed suicide in her car, presumably by carbon-monoxide poisoning. There were a number of stories of where this had taken place. One story said that she had done it either in the carport or at the back of the house.

The sequel to the episode of the lady came about six months later. It was late fall or winter and my husband was involved in amateur sports in Vancouver. He invited two of his cohorts to dinner. One of them brought his wife and the other his girlfriend. The girlfriend walked into the house looking white and somewhat disturbed. She was very quiet through most of the evening. We put it down to the fact that possibly she had not wanted to come to an evening that would, in all likelihood, be devoted to sports talk.

However, sitting comfortably in the living-room after dinner, over coffee and liqueurs, we talked about many things. The conversation turned to the subject of _déjà vu_ and ghosts. My husband suddenly said that I had seen a ghost in that very house. The girl almost sat up in her chair and became more animated, wanting to know all the details. It finally emerged that she had been very close to one of her lady teachers during the latter part of her high-school years, and had often visited the teacher at her house, which she shared with another lady. The teacher had committed suicide, and this had badly shaken the student. Her boyfriend had told her only that they were invited out for dinner, not where they were going, and it was not until she was walking up the garden path to our front door that she realized she was revisiting the teacher's old house. She had not been there since the suicide. This was the reason for the white face. She had been very quiet because she did not know whether or not we knew about what had happened and she did not want to be the one to tell us. Her description of the schoolteacher fit the appearance of the lady, both in body and in attitude.

We obtained no further information, as our guests departed soon after the revelation. We had been so excited by what the girl had said that we never even thought to ask for such details as the lady's name or the year that it had all happened.

We still live in the house, although we have made many changes over the years. These included closing doorways and extending the building. We have had no further manifestations since that one occurrence. My daughter affectionately describes the lady as Mum's ghost.

The striking thing about the episode is the clarity of the lady and the amount of detail I was able to amass during the few seconds — probably fewer than ten — that it lasted. The feeling it left with me was that we had been checked out and found to be satisfactory, both in character and in our attitude to the house. The schoolteacher had apparently been very house-proud. I had the feeling that she left happy.

The other thing that occurs to me is that this is the first time I have written a description of the occurrence since it happened. Yet everything is still very clear. We have told some friends about the incident, and their reactions vary from total disbelief to not wanting to return to the house until we can assure them that the lady has not returned.

I might add that both my husband and I are scientists. Our scientific training makes us wary of things that are not tangible; although we are reluctant to jump to conclusions without solid evidence, we must be flexible because we need to be able to countenance research experiments that produce results different from those anticipated. We have to be curious to know why something is happening.

We were somewhat skeptical of ghosts until the incident of the lady. My husband, I believe, is not quite sure what to think — he knows that I saw something, judging from my appearance at the dining-room table, but he saw nothing himself. I would say that my husband would probably consider himself a skeptic, but not a non-believer about ghosts, etc. He does not discount their occurrence, but has not had any experiences himself. I have to count myself as a believer in extraordinary experiences, if only because of "my lady."

I do not believe that the experience has changed our lives at all. The topic has come up only a handful of times during the last fifteen years, usually during one of those wide-ranging, after-dinner conversations that touch on all kinds of topics. I am not sure why, except one does get the feeling that some people will ridicule such an experience, while others seem to be terrified of the very thought of ghosts!

Incidentally, my daughter, when she learned about the incident, did not seem to be worried, upset, or frightened at the thought that her mother had once seen a lady in the house. In fact, she rather seems to wish that it would happen again!

The Chinese Ghost

Allan Blue is a restaurateur, now retired, who opened an exclusive restaurant near Point Grey in Vancouver. He learned to his surprise that the building was haunted. Some years later he moved to Toronto where he assumed the management of an established restaurant, Cherry Hill House, which also proved to be haunted. Perhaps there is something about Allan Blue that brings the spirits out of the woodwork! Here is his account of his experiences in the Vancouver restaurant.

———

Some years ago, when I lived in Vancouver, a friend from Birmingham, England, and I bought an old corner store, with the thought of turning it into a small but exclusive restaurant. After nearly six months of renovations and getting the proper permits, we were finally able to open.

Fortunately, we were well-received by the public, especially since we were located in an area near the university where interesting people lived who had little money but had the taste for the unusual in dining.

To keep our costs down, we both lived above the dining-room in what had, years earlier, been an apartment that housed the operators and family of the greengrocers when the building had been viable as that. We kept our day jobs, just in case the venture turned out badly.

Because of the long hours, both at work and at the restaurant, I used to really value my sleep. I appreciated the convenience of being able to run upstairs either to sleep or to catnap. Often I would have fitful dreams and nightmares. I put these down to fatigue. Perhaps they were the result of eating very late at night and of trying out new dishes and new seasonings for the chef.

One dream that persisted was the one of an elderly Chinese gentleman who seemed to appear at the foot of my bed. He just stood there, smiling serenely at me, so I never really got frightened or anything. In the morning I would always remember this one dream and would put it down to eating late.

The man in the dream always looked the same, however: short, nearly bald, chubby, and leaning on a cane. No one I could recall from real life. Oh, well!

After nearly a year in business, I realized that the restaurant was going to be successful, so I was able to give up my day job and concentrate full-time on the business. We each took apartments elsewhere and used the upstairs for the storage of extra chairs and things.

One evening we had a small group of foreign students as the last table of the evening. I found their conversation to be animated and very interesting, so I relaxed with a cognac at their table. We discussed various aspects of life in the places from which each of them had come. Finding that one of them had lived in Birmingham, England, after being brought up in Barbados, I went to the kitchen and told Peter, the chef, who was a "Brummie," as they're known, to come and join us. He did and we talked.

After an enjoyable visit, the group went to leave. They were saying their goodbyes in the vestibule, when the one from the Caribbean asked who helped Peter in the kitchen. Peter replied that he worked alone, since the place was small and staff was still, at this time, an expensive luxury.

Then the customer said, "Well, who was that nice old gentleman that we noticed standing at the foot of the stairs?"

We looked at one another and asked him to describe the person he saw. His answer nearly floored us both. (I had told Peter several times about the recurring dream I had when I had lived upstairs.) "The man was a friendly, smiling, old Oriental, leaning on a cane. My assumption was that he might work in some capacity for you. I remember he was wearing old-fashioned suspenders, too."

When he said that, a real chill came across me, as the suspenders touched off a long-forgotten memory of the man I had seen so often in my dreaming!

The others in the group were waiting with the door open and shouting for their friend to hurry and come. We said our goodnights and locked the door, then sat down for another cognac, while trying to understand just what had happened. We couldn't explain it, so we left it for another day when we were not so tired.

Several days later I made a point of going to several of the shops in the area, questioning the owners about the history of our building. What I had suspected was true. A Chinese man by the name of Lee had owned the store for over fifty years. He had raised a family of eight in the upstairs apartment. All had gone on to do well in other fields, while Mr. and Mrs. Lee continued to run the store and live above it.

One neighbour added the detail that Mr. Lee had passed away in his sleep in his bedroom, which was the very room I had used to sleep in. Mr. Lee had been eighty-three at the time. I asked the man to describe Mr. Lee to me....

You know his reply!

The "Twilight Zone" Truck Stop

This is one of the eeriest stories that I have yet encountered. The story is told by Phyllis Griffiths of Victoria, British Columbia. In it she recalls what happened late one night on an ill-used highway when she, her husband Don, their two sons, and the family dog drove their station wagon into a very peculiar Texaco Truck Stop. What they experienced may well have been a hallucination, but if so, it was a most vivid one and common to all of them. Phyllis Griffiths recalled the experience eleven years later in these words:

In March of 1978, we were returning to our home in Lethbridge, Alberta, after spending Easter Week visiting relatives on Vancouver

Island. This was a trip that the family had taken many times before, and the route we usually followed was first along Highway 1, the northern route, and then south from Calgary. This time, we decided, just for a change of pace, that we would take Highway 3. We had not taken this southern highway before when returning from Vancouver Island.

As usual with return trips, this one was to be driven straight through. But the route was unfamiliar to us, and the southern route was taking much longer than the familiar, northern route. Our two young sons slept cuddled up to their dog in the back seat of the family station wagon. My husband and I drove through the night and into the early hours of the next day without a rest.

At two-thirty in the morning we drove into the town of Creston, British Columbia. The only place open at that early hour was a tiny service station, where we stopped to refuel the car. Tired as we were, we had no choice but to drive on. There was no money for a motel room, nor were there campgrounds in the area.

Relief was found about half way between Creston and Cranbrook. It took the form of an old Texaco Truck Stop that we were approaching. It was on the north side of the highway, Highway 3, but it was located in the middle of nowhere. It was a totally unexpected sight, but a very welcome one.

The Texaco Truck Stop had an unusual location, but it also had an unusual appearance. The large old Texaco sign was a solid sign lit by spotlights mounted on top and focused on the painted surface. The gas pumps were also old-fashioned, and they dispensed good old Fire Chief and Sky Chief gasoline. There was a diesel pump at the side, but no pumps for unleaded gas were in sight.

The station itself looked as if it had not changed one bit since the year 1960. Even the semi-trailer unit, idling in the truck lot to one side, was of an early sixties vintage. Everything looked strange indeed. Was this a scene from Rod Serling's "Twilight Zone"?

Nevertheless, my husband and I, tired and thirsty as we were, drove in, pulled up under the pump lights, got out of the car, and locked it. We left our two children asleep in the back seat of the car.

The inside of the restaurant matched the outside to such a degree that everything felt spooky. The interior was frozen in time in the year 1960, yet the decor showed none of the wear and tear that would be found after nearly twenty years of use. We could see nothing that was out of place. There was nothing new or modern about the appointments or the personnel. The waitress was dressed in period clothes, as was the driver of the semi parked in the yard.

The price of the coffee was all of a dime a cup, and a placard advertised the price of a piece of pie as a quarter. The music blaring from the radio dated from the late fifties, and the deejay introduced the songs without once referring to the period or to any item of news. No calendar was in sight. But the coffee was good and was appreciated. We felt uneasy in the place, so we were not unhappy to be out and on the road for home once more.

We had driven this stretch of Highway 3 on previous occasions, but it had always been in daylight and heading in the other direction. We had never taken it at night or while returning from Vancouver Island. We had memorized the location of every truck stop on Highway 3, and we thought we knew the location of all the truck stops that were open twenty-four hours a day on this highway as well. But never before had we seen this one. Nor did we ever see it again.

The visit left us with an eerie feeling. Try as we might, we could not shake it off. We asked those of our friends and relatives who occasionally travelled that stretch of Highway 3 if they were familiar with the old Texaco Truck Stop. No one knew anything about it. Everyone was of the opinion that there was no such establishment between Lethbridge, Alberta, and Hope, British Columbia.

The only thing that we could do was re-drive that stretch of highway in broad daylight and watch out for it to see for ourselves whether or not the place really existed. Some months later we did just that. We retravelled Highway 3. Midway between Cranbrook and Creston, on the north side of the road, we found the place where we had stopped that eerie night.

The building had long been boarded over. The presence of the pumps was marked only by their cement bases. The same was true of the Texaco signpost. The yard where the semi had sat was overgrown with bush and with aspen poplars that were twenty or more feet in height. It had been many years since that particular service station had pumped gas or served coffee at a dime a cup. But my husband and I know that the old Truck Stop had been open for business that lonely March night in 1978, when a weary family had stopped — in need of a cup of coffee and a bit of rest.

THE NORTH

Mackenzie River Ghost

The story of the Mackenzie River Ghost is a particular favourite of mine. There are four reasons why it is close to my heart — and head.

The story is very old. It goes back to the 1850s. That may not be old for the tales told of haunted castles in England and Scotland, which go back to the fifteenth and sixteenth centuries, but it is ancient for Canada.

The story is well-established. Many stories are told and retold based on flimsy evidence. We have the story of the Mackenzie River in the words of Roderick MacFarlane, who witnessed the events that he describes. Firsthand accounts make compelling reading.

The story is widely known. Not only is it widely known, but for many years it was one of a handful of ghost stories set in Canada that was known at all. Over the last century, MacFarlane's account has appeared in a number of books, but its most notable appearance was in *Lord Halifax's Ghost Book: A Collection of Stories of Haunted Houses, Apparitions and Supernatural Occurrences Made by Charles Lindley, Viscount Halifax* (1936). This collection of true-life ghost stories was widely read in its day and has influenced most subsequent collections of such stories.

The story is set in the Canadian North. The Northwest Territories would seem to be an unlikely locale for a story of a haunting, yet this one is perfectly credible in its setting.

Read on....

It all began with the death of Augustus Richard Peers. A fur trader and post manager for the Hudson's Bay Company, Peers was only thirty-three years old and in good health when he died on March 15, 1853, at Fort McPherson, District of Mackenzie, Northwest Territories.

The reason for his death is not recorded; there is no reason to suspect foul play, as he had no known enemies among his fellow traders and he was popular with the Indians who visited the trading post. He was happily married with two children.

Peers had made it known to his wife and friends that in the event of his death he did not want his bones to lie permanently at Fort

McPherson. Nonetheless they were buried at Fort McPherson and they rested there until the autumn of 1859. Then, at the request of his widow, who had by now remarried, it was decided that the long-delayed transfer of Peers's remains would take place that winter. To this end Charles P. Gaudet agreed to convey the body by dog sled and train some three hundred miles along the Mackenzie River to Fort Good Hope. Roderick MacFarlane was in charge of that fort, and he agreed to accompany the body the journey of some six hundred miles to Fort Simpson, its final destination.

Gaudet exhumed Peers's body from the frozen ground and had it transferred to a new coffin. The rather large coffin was secured by moose skin and rope to a dog sled. It was bulky and Gaudet had some difficulties conducting the dog sled and train over the tossed-up ice along the banks of the Mackenzie River. Nevertheless, Gaudet arrived with his consignment at Fort Good Hope on March 1, 1860, and he delivered the body to MacFarlane.

MacFarlane outfitted two dog sleds and set out through the snow for Fort Simpson. The large coffin was conveyed by one team of three dogs conducted by Michel Thomas, an Iroquois from Caughnawaga, near Montreal. The second team led by Nicol Taylor, a former employee of Peers, conveyed the bedding, utensils, and provisions. MacFarlane accompanied the two teams on snowshoes. It took them seven days to cover two hundred miles between Fort Good Hope and Fort Norman. Fort Norman was the halfway mark between the departure point of Fort McPherson and the destination point of Fort Simpson. Peers's remains were about halfway home. So far it was tough sledding, but nothing untoward had happened.

At Fort Norman, Nicol Taylor pointed out that the tossed-up ice was an impediment that would only increase and the only way to continue south was to remove the body from the large coffin and secure Peers's remains to the sled. MacFarlane agreed and the transfer was effected. Fresh animals were obtained and a new driver, Michel Iroquois, was engaged. Four men — Michel Iroquois, Michel Thomas, Nicol Taylor, and Roderick MacFarlane — set out on the last and longest leg of their trek.

MacFarlane described a typical day of their trek: "Here it may be briefly stated that we got under way by four o'clock in the morning; dined at some convenient spot about noon, and after an hour's rest, resumed our march until sunset, when we laid up for the night, generally in a pine bluff on the top or close to an immediate bank of the river." MacFarlane went on to describe how they spent an hour setting up camp, clearing away the snow, and collecting pine brush and firewood for cooking and warming purposes. Another hour was spent over supper and feeding the dogs. It was an exhausting routine. "The train carrying the body of the deceased was invariably hauled up and placed for the night in the immediate rear of our encampment." The dogs displayed no interest in the corpse.

About sunset on the seventh anniversary of Peers's death, March 15, 1860, the men left the two dog trains on the ice of the Mackenzie River, unharnessed the dogs, and climbed with some difficulty the thirty-foot river banks in search of a suitable campground. Ten or so minutes later, the dogs began to bark. Their barking suggested that they had spotted someone approaching them. But there were no Indians or traders in the vicinity. Over the sound of the barking MacFarlane and the others distinctly heard someone call out the order "*Marché!*"

MacFarlane later noted that the French word for "March!" was used throughout the Northwest Territories by masters to urge their dogs onward. He then wrote, "It seemed to have been uttered by someone at the foot of the bank who wished to drive away the dogs in his path, and we all left off work in order to see who the stranger was; but as no one appeared in sight, Michel Thomas and myself proceeded to the aforesaid summit, where, to our astonishment, no man was visible, while the dogs were seen surrounding the body train at a distance of several feet, and still apparently excited at something. We had to call them repeatedly before they gave up barking." MacFarlane then ordered the men to haul both the baggage sled and the body sled up the icy embankment for the night.

Three days later, while camping, the four men again left the body on its sled on the frozen river, climbing the icy embankment to find a suitable place to make camp. Again from down below they heard the dogs bark and the clear call "*Marché!*" They were alarmed, and checked for the tracks of some intruder, but found none. They decided, however, to haul the body sled up the embankment for the night. The next morning, they examined the spot where the body sled had rested, and discovered that a wolverine had been there during the night. "To those who know the power of this destructive animal," wrote

MacFarlane, "I need not say that he would have played havoc with the aforesaid remains."

It was with relief that on March 21, 1860, the four men, the body, the provisions, and the dogs reached Fort Simpson. Two days later the body was buried in the graveyard there. MacFarlane and Taylor told the story of hearing the clear calls of "*Marché!*" and attending to the protection of the body to Bernard R. Ross, the chief trader of the district. Ross was quite interested, as he had been a close friend of Peers. "Mr. Ross was a good mimic and had an excellent memory," MacFarlane wrote. "He was asked to utter the word *marché* in the voice of the deceased, and while I at once recognized the tone as similar to that heard by us at our encampment on the fifteenth of March, Mr. Taylor had no doubt whatever on the subject."

That night MacFarlane and Ross retired for the night after discussing the unusual occurrences. But neither MacFarlane nor Ross could sleep. MacFarlane explained, "I became overpoweringly conscious of what struck me then and since to have been the spiritual or supernatural presence of the late Mr. Peers. The feeling, however, came on so very suddenly and scaringly that I instantly covered my face with the blanket and remained speechless. After an interval of perhaps only a few seconds Mr. Ross (whose voice had also ceased) in a somewhat excited tone asked me if I had experienced a very peculiar sensation. I answered that I had and described the feeling, which he assured me agreed exactly with what he himself had just undergone." MacFarlane was distressed, especially as neither he nor Ross had partaken of wines, spirits, or anything else that could have produced these sensations.

A practical man, MacFarlane pondered the problem for some time. He eventually came to the conclusion that the spirit of the dead Peers had warned them that his mortal remains were in danger on two occasions. On the first occasion, the night of March 15, the weather was somewhat mild and the scent of the body may have attracted the interest of the dogs. Hence the warning. On the second occasion, the night of March 18, there was danger to the body from the wolverine. Dangers on both occasions were avoided by the call of "*Marché!*" which led the men to haul the body to higher ground.

MacFarlane found this to be the sole explanation to fit the facts. He concluded, "I leave it to others, if they can, to give a reasonable account or explanation of the facts I have here stated."

Thus ends the thousand-mile journey of the mortal remains of Augustus Richard Peers, the fur trade and post manager for the Hudson's Bay Company, whose spirit ensured that his wish to be buried at Fort Simpson came true.

Spirit Rapping in the Far North

The following account was written with considerable coyness. It concerns a poltergeist that was encountered in the part of the world that today is called the Yukon Territory. The account was first published in 1866.

Under this heading we mention some curious facts which occurred at the Hudson's Bay Company Fort on the Youcon [Yukon] River, in Russian America. The quiet and monotony of life at that far off Northern Post was rudely disturbed by what a Trance Medium would call "Manifestations," said manifestations consisting in the kicking up of a most unseemly row in all the spare rooms of the Fort, and — if such an expression can be properly applied to spiritual visitants — raising Cain generally.

The eccentric conduct on the part of the Spirits was of course calculated to exercise the minds of the matter of fact people of the Fort, to a very great extent, and in fact caused such a feeling as was likely to result in the Fort's being abandoned. Such was the state of affairs when we mentioned the subject before, but we have since learned that a diversion has occurred in favour of the Fort people.

The time came when Mr. Jones, the Gentleman in charge, left the Fort for Canada by way of this Settlement, and much to the surprise and pleasure of the people at the Fort and doubtless much to the disgust of Mr. J. the Spirits left with him; not only left with him, but as we hear, stuck to him, like bad luck, or the itch till he arrived here.

On board the York Boats in which a greater part of the journey was performed, the Spirits, not having the field to bang stove pipes, and smash chairs, which they enjoyed at the Youcon, had to content themselves with scratchings on the masthead, raps on the keel, which raps and scratchings, with an occasional smashing of a trunk, continued during the whole of the voyage.

The voyageurs unanimously voted the manifestations to be "le diable pour le sure" and doubtless had they been at all acquainted with a certain incident in the life of one of the Old Testament worthies, would have drawn some strange conclusions from the resemblance which the name of Jones bears to that of Jonah. Mr. Jones, the Gentleman whom the Spirits seem so persistently to pursue, left here by way of St. Paul for Canada, and we are a little curious to know whether these polar Ghosts have continued their pranks in the stage coaches, Steamboats, and Railroads of the neighbouring Republic.

The Frozen City of the Yukon

Entries from the journals of explorers of the Far North abound in detailed descriptions of the rich and strange shapes assumed in the eyes of the beholders by glaciers, clouds, icebergs, crevasses, hillocks, mounds, frozen lakes, snowdrifts, etc. The air of the Arctic, so cold and crystal clear, tricks the eye at every turn. It generates images and illusions of its own, creating long-lasting mirages and visions.

The Silent City of Alaska is one such illusion; another is the Phantom City of Glacier Bay. Both of these mirages occur in Alaska. In Canada, there is the Frozen City of the Yukon. According to the account of this report, somewhere amid the frozen vastness of the Yukon there exists an entire city, which was erected in the distant past by a civilized people who possessed a high degree of technology and artistry who then abandoned, under mysterious circumstances, their marvellous city. Yet it remains amid the ice and snow of the Yukon, "hidden in wonder," to press into use a phrase from a poem written about the Far North by the late F.R. Scott.

The descriptions of silent and phantom cities are never far removed from the equally dramatic accounts by later travellers of actual cities preserved in ice. Travellers' tales —especially tall tales told by gold prospectors — are all to the point. It is possible that this account of the Frozen City of the Yukon is based on the narrator's own personal experience; the odds are that the narrative owes its existence to one man's imagination. Yet this frozen city, chanced upon by an American prospector and his Indian helper, may remain there, somewhere in the Yukon, to this day....

The account is taken from *The Wonders of Alaska* (San Francisco: The Bancroft Company, 1890) by Alexander Badlam, who introduced the story with these words: "Inasmuch as I have taken pains to give the imaginary wonders of Alaska to the public, it is a source of pleasure to present the latest in the way of Silent and Phantom Cities. From the telegraphic news published in the San Francisco *Examiner*, it seems that a man named George Kershon joined a party of miners who were bent on exploring the ice-bound secrets of Alaska. In an interview Mr. Kershon said:"

In the summer of 1888, I was one of the party who left here to go north prospecting. At Juneau we purchased a small sloop to take our outfit up to the Yukon, which we reached after many weeks of toil. I disagreed with my partners and engaged an Indian canoe with two Indians, and started to prospect along an unknown fork of the Yukon River. We had a terrible time. The stream narrowed in between high cliffs and shot with dizzy swiftness down the gulches, making it necessary to tow the canoe by means of a line from the banks, two doing this while the third man rested. Progress was necessarily slow, and for many days we toiled before the first range of cliffs and mountains was passed. Once a hundred-foot water-fall barred us, and it took three days to get around it.

After this it was a bit easier. The river broadened out and the country was more level. The banks were well wooded and game was plentiful. We kept on like this, always going north, when, after six weeks, a range of mountains was sighted; I believed this to be the head of the river, and passed on to reach it before the cold weather set in. Snow was now falling very often, and it was evident that the short summer was nearly done. At length we reached the wild country again, and the stream which had been sub-dividing itself into the lesser ones soon became too difficult to navigate. This was almost at the foot of the range of mountains spoken of. Here we determined to camp for the winter, and good quarters were found. Everything was made snug, as the weather up there is something awful, but we were in a deep ravine, overhung by high cliffs, which broke the fury of the winds, and the best was made of it. Game was plentiful, and large quantities of elk and deer were shot and frozen for use through the long winter months.

Before long the cold came, and at times it was impossible to stir from cover; especially was this the case when the terrible winds blew. At other times it was fairly comfortable, although the lack of sun made it gloomy enough. Toward the end of winter it began to get lighter and the gales were less frequent.

One day I determined to try and scale one of the mountains near us, as I got so tired and weary of being penned up in such a confined place. This idea I put before the Indians. One of them said he would go with me; the other would not risk it, so he was left in camp. A storm shortly arose, blowing heavily for three days, but as soon as the weather had settled, the Indian and myself started off on our trip.

We went right up the line of the frozen river, which, being a solid mass of ice, made a good roadway. Following this for about twenty miles, at a pretty steep rise, we reached a plateau between the foothills and high range. Here the stream ended, and we started to climb one of the big hills. After a lot of hard work we reached a point near the summit. A wonderful view was had from here, but the strangest thing was a city in one of the valleys below. You may depend upon it, I was surprised to see it. At first I thought it was some fantastic arrangement of ice and which had assumed the form of a city, but examination with the glass showed that such was not the case, it being too regular in appearance. It was a city sure enough. Determined to see more of it, I commenced to work downwards, although the Indian was rather frightened, he evidently not considered it "good medicine." After several hours of hard work I reached the outskirts of this mysterious city, and found that the place was laid out in streets, with blocks of strange-looking buildings, what appeared to be mosques, towers, ports, etc., and every evidence of having been built by art. The whole was not of solid ice, though it seemed to be, but blows from a hatchet on one of the walls disclosed the fact that beneath this barrier of ice was some sort of building material. It looked to be wood, but of a stone-like hardness and apparently petrified. The silence around the place was something ghostly. Not the slightest sound broke the awful stillness of the place which, added to the weird look of the empty streets, made it gruesome enough. I soon got tired of investigating the city, as the streets were blocked in many places with huge masses of ice, rendering passage almost impossible. The Indian, too, became uneasy, and we started on the return trip, reaching home the next day, tired but satisfied that we had been the first men to gaze on that silent city for centuries.

After spring broke I made some strikes in nugget gold at the head-waters of the river, working with the Indians through the summer months, leaving camp for the Yukon about the end of August. We reached that river all right, the trip down being easy, and in due time I got back to Juno, where I took the steamer for the south.

It was while I was at Juno I saw a newspaper with an account of the mirage seen at Muir Glacier. I did not make any allusions to this, though, as I did not think any one would believe me, but I am positive that the mirage of Muir Glacier is the reflection of the frozen city found by me. In accounting for the presence of this wonderful reflected city I'll have to leave to abler heads. You might ask me how the ruins of big cities came in the interior of Central America. They are there, but who built them nobody knows. Perhaps at one time it was not so cold north as it is now.

Alexander Badlam continued:

This ended Mr. Kershon's story, told with an air of truth that made it evident that he had truly seen the things he said he did.

The public have been shown the entire history of the Silent City, the Phantom City and the reflected-city business last mentioned and they may draw their own conclusions. That mirages exist in Alaska as well as on the great deserts, and are easily accounted for by the condition of the atmosphere, is a fact; but a photograph of Bristol, another by Mr. Taber's artist and still another picture shown in a pan of quicksilver, with this last candidate for fame as the discoverer of a real deserted city, I think will rank high among Baron Munchausen's fairy tales, and the public who are easily amused will doubtless look upon these pleasantries from their own standpoint in accordance with the intelligence they possess and in the extent of their credulity.

Ghost Ship of the Arctic Sea

The SS *Baychimo*, it is said, is the only derelict in history to repeatedly defy the crushing ice packs year after year and escape destruction or even severe damage.

That was the opinion of researcher Vincent Gaddis, writing in his book *Invisible Horizons: Mysteries of the Sea*. He was describing the famed vessel that was fated to sail without crew the frigid waters of the Beaufort Sea.

The *Baychimo* was a 1,300-ton, steel-clad, twin-screw steamer in the fleet of fur ships owned and operated by the Hudson's Bay Company. It was launched in 1921 and it proved seaworthy and lucky for ten years. Then, on October 1, 1931, it was caught in ice off the coast of Wainwright, Alaska. The captain and the crew of sixteen abandoned the vessel and set up a winter camp close by, where they could keep an eye on their ship and its cargo, a fortune in bundled fur. They waited for the warm weather to thaw the ice.

But fate had another future in store for the *Baychimo*. On November 2, a storm loosened the ice and the vessel snapped its moorings and drifted off. An Eskimo hunter spotted it forty-five miles southwest of its former position. The crew trekked to the new location and was successful in off-loading the furs before the ship again slipped its moorings. Five months later prospectors came upon the wandering vessel near Herschel Island and boarded it. It was boarded again, passing Point Barrow, in 1933. In fact, it was seen regularly from year to year, and was last boarded in November 1939, when it was found to be still seaworthy and still crewless.

"As far as I can determine," wrote Gaddis in 1965, "the *Baychimo* was last sighted by Eskimos in March, 1956, in the Beaufort Sea, moving north and still apparently seaworthy, riding the sea as if an expert mariner was at her helm. Her story has no parallel. No other derelict in modern times has been known to survive the ice for more than two years. The *Baychimo* has been around, crewless, for twenty-five years!"

Nothing further is known of the fate of this remarkable vessel. It remains the Ghost Ship of the Arctic Sea.

The Village of the Dead

The sign of a good story is that it never dies. Even if it is known to be false, even if it is known to be a hoax, it lingers in the memory and appeals to the imagination.

The Village of the Dead is the tale of a mystery that is too good to die. It packs so much appeal because the tale is set in an inaccessible part of the country — on the shore of Lake Angikuni in the District of

Keewatin, Nunavut, some eight hundred kilometres northwest of Churchill, Manitoba. Another reason for its appeal is that it concerns the Inuit, who are seen by southerners to be a vanishing race. Certainly these are two facts that led credence to the Village of the Dead.

Readers of the Halifax *Herald* and other North American newspapers were treated to a fantastic story on November 29, 1930. The headline told it all:

Tribe Lost in Barrens of North
Village of Dead Found by Wandering Trapper, Joe Labelle

It was written by "special correspondent" Emmett E. Kelleher, from The Pas, Manitoba, and it began like this: "The northern lights have seen queer sights — as the much-quoted Robert W. Service remarks — and the everlasting silence of the regions under the Arctic Circle cloaks some strange mysteries. But the northern lights do not tell of the queer sights, nor does the Arctic silence get vocal about its mysteries. There is nothing to do, usually, but guess." Kelleher continued:

Far up in the heart of one of the most lonely places on earth — in the Lake Angikuni country, 500 miles northwest of the port of Churchill, on Hudson Bay — a whole tribe of Eskimos has vanished. Somewhere, somehow, the endless desolation of Canada's northern Barren Lands has swallowed up 25 men, women and children. It is one of the most puzzling mysteries that has ever come down out of the Arctic. The news of it has just reached The Pas, on the fringe of civilization.

Kelleher recounted the experience of "one Joe Labelle, a roving trapper of the Barren Lands," who came upon the tribe's abandoned camp. Its caribou-skin tents were still standing. Inside were the occupant's prized possessions, including cooking utensils and rifles. "There was no sign of violence, no sign of trouble. The place was simply empty."

According to Kelleher, the officers of the Royal Canadian Mounted Police (which he called by its old name, the North-West Mounted Police) "have taken up the hunt and white trappers have been asked to be on the lookout." Then Kelleher waxed eloquent:

Joe Labelle admits that stumbling on the abandoned village gave him the creeps. A man doesn't get the creeps readily when he spends months at a time trudging by his lone across the Barren Lands, where there is never a house or a human being or anything to break the white-rimmed silence; but Joe Labelle got creepy, just the same. The empty sky and the silent, rocky plain held a mystery, and the trapper didn't like it.

The sense of mystery deepened when Labelle came upon two half-starved Husky dogs and the bodies of seven dead dogs, and his thoughts turned darker:

There were six tents made out of skin.... I'll admit that when I went in the first tent I was a little jumpy. Just looking around, I could see the place hadn't known any human life for months, and I expected to find corpses inside. But there was nothing there but the personal belongings of a family. A couple of deer parkas (skin coats) were in one corner. Fish and deer bones were scattered about. There were a few pairs of boots, and an iron pot, greasy and black. Under one of the parkas I found a rifle. It had been there so long it was all rusty. The whole thing looked as if it had been left just that way by people who expected to come back. But they hadn't come back.

I went outside and looked over the rest of the camp. I tell you, I was puzzled. I figured there had been about 25 people in the camp, but all signs showed the place hadn't been lived in for nearly 12 months. As I strolled about, with those two walking skeletons of dogs following me, I found the other tents in a similar condition.

I tried to figure out where those Eskimos had gone. They hadn't moved to a new territory, or they would have taken their equipment, especially their guns and their dogs. Then I thought of the Eskimos' "evil spirit" Tornrark, who has an ugly man's face with two long tusks sticking up from each side of the nose. The natives live in fear of Tornrark, and they wear charms to ward him off. I thought about Tornrark, and I had to make an effort to put the picture out of my mind.

Labelle made an even more surprising discovery:

Then I found one of the most puzzling things of all. It was an Eskimo grave, with a cairn built of stones. But for some reason the grave had been opened. The stones had been pulled off of one side and there was nothing inside the cairn at all. I had no way of telling when it had been opened, or what had been done with the body it had once contained. And I couldn't figure out why it had been desecrated.

I stayed around all afternoon, trying to figure things out. There were no signs of any struggle. Everything looked peaceful. But the air seemed deadly. I caught a few fish out of the lake and gave them to the two dogs, and then moved on. I didn't want to spend a night there.

So that is the story of the Village of the Dead.

The eerie tale attracted the attention of broadcaster and journalist Frank Edwards, who added the following flight of rhetoric: "Months of patient and far-flung investigation failed to produce a single trace of any member who had lived in the deserted village of Angikuni. The Mounted Police filed it as unsolved ... and so it remained."

These sentences come from the chapter called "The Vanishing Village" in Edwards's book *Stranger than Science* (1959). They are so wide of the mark as to be marvels of their own. The truth, which is much more interesting than Joe Labelle's tall tale and Kelleher's journalistic hoax, is that within two months of its publication, the Royal Canadian Mounted Police, which patrols the Northwest Territories, had debunked the tale in all its particulars.

After Kelleher's story appeared in the Halifax *Herald* and other newspapers, the RCMP received inquiries from the general public. On January 17, 1931, Commissioner Cortland Starnes made public the internal report of Sergeant J. Nelson of The Pas detachment. On January 5, 1931, Sergeant Nelson wrote: "I have made diligent enquiries from different sources but can find no foundation for this story." Then he noted:

In conversation with Mr. D. Simons, recently, who operates a trading post at Windy Lake, N.W.T., and has just returned from visiting his Post by plane; he doubts the suggestion that any such calamity has occurred, as no doubt there would be reports from reliable white trappers and Eskimos of that district.

Joe Labelle the trapper who is alleged to have related the story to Emmett E. Kelleher, the correspondent, is considered a new-comer in this country. The Manitoba records show this to be his first season, that he has taken out a trapping licence, he is located on some of the lakes north of Flin Flon, and doubts are expressed as to whether he has ever been in the Territories.

The illustration which depicts "The Village of the Dead" is a photograph which was taken by an ex-member of this Force, Mr. P. Rose, while stationed at Fort Churchill in 1909, and is now living in The Pas. I have compared the negative in Mr. Rose's possession and the illustration and find them identical. Some time ago Mr. Kelleher was visiting Mr. Rose and was looking over some photos of the North, when he came to a photo which is depicted as "The Village of the Dead" in the illustration, he asked to borrow it, to get a copy for his album, later returning the negative to Mr. Rose....

From my own knowledge of the correspondent, I consider the whole story fiction. Mr. Kelleher is in the habit of writing colourful stories of the North, and very little credence can be given to his articles. At present he is visiting in the east, and should he return to The Pas, I will interview him regarding the above matter.

There is no information that Kelleher ever returned to The Pas, "the scene of the crime." Whether or not he did, Sgt. Nelson "got his man."

The most thorough-going debunking of the story was Dwight Whalen's "Vanished Village Revisited" published in *Fate Magazine*, November 1976. Whalen, a researcher in Niagara Falls, Ontario, wrote to all the appropriate authorities and could find no independent corroboration of Kelleher's story. He concluded, perhaps with some regret, "Thus, the case for the vanished village rests upon the story of an inexperienced trapper told to an imaginative and not too conscientious newsman."

Yet the tale continues to be told and retold. Perhaps its most surprising quality is its eerie stillness. In the finest of ghost stories, the reader faces the consequences of the act of dissolution, being forced to imaginatively reconstruct the causes. So the supernatural is seldom directly experienced but is kept at bay, at a distance. At the heart of the Lake Angikuni mystery lies a sense of abandonment and a scene of disaster and ruin. In its presentation of an eerie stillness, it rivals the greatest of all the mysteries of the sea, the abandonment on the high seas of the Nova Scotia-built vessel, the *Mary Celeste*. No doubt the story of "The Village of the Dead" will be told and retold as long as there is a Dominion of Canada.

Sources

Sources for the stories in this book are arranged in two sections.

Section One offers the reader the most readily available sources for the ghost stories in this book. In most instances, the information provided leads to such primary source material as exists. Many stories have generated reams of commentary; other stories derive from a single source, one that may be unique to the present book.

Section Two comprises a bibliography of contemporary Canadian collections of told-as-true ghost stories along with a handful of non-current books of continuing interest. Readers interested in further titles are directed to the bibliography (limited to 123 titles) included in my tome *Mysterious Canada* (1988). The present bibliography scants folklore, so the scholar should check Edith Fowke and Carole Henderson Carpenter's *A Bibliography of Canadian Folklore in English* (1981). Also relevant is George M. Eberhart's *A Geo-Bibliography of Anomalies* (1980). It took much effort, but I resisted the impulse to add to this bibliography entries for ghost stories of a fictional nature. Readers of real-life ghosts stories are not, I have found, regular readers of fantastic fiction. (I wonder if there is a negative correlation.) Anyway, for the fiction of horror and terror, check *Not to Be Taken at Night* (1981), the first anthology of Canadian stories, which I co-edited with Michael Richardson, as well as anthologies edited by David Skene-Melvin, Don Hutchison, and Alberto Manguel.

Section One

Maritimes

1. The Fairy Companion

W.Y. Evans-Wentz, *The Fairy-Faith in Celtic Countries* (London: Henry Frowde, 1911; Gerrards Cross, Bucks.: Colin Smythe, 1977).

2. A Night with the Fairies

Barbara Rieti, *Strange Terrain: The Fairy World in Newfoundland* (St. John's: ISER, 1991).

3. The Phantom Trapper

John Robert Colombo, *Mysterious Canada: Strange Sights, Extraordinary Events, and Peculiar Places* (Toronto: Doubleday, 1988).

4. The Fire-Ship of Northumberland Strait

Colombo, *Mysterious Canada*.

Edward D. Ives, "The Burning Ship of the Northumberland Strait: Some Notes on that Apparition," *Northeast Folklore*, Vol. 2, 1959.

5. The Phantom Ship of the Bay of Chaleur

Colombo, *Mysterious Canada*.

Edith Fowke, Unpublished research.

6. The Grey Lady of Annapolis Royal

Colombo, *Mysterious Canada*.

7. The Teazer Light

Colombo, *Mysterious Canada*.

8. The Battle in the Sky

Edith Fowke, Unpublished research.

Sterling Ramsay, *Folklore, Prince Edward Island* (Charlottetown: Square Deal, 1974).

9. The Ghost of Dr. Copeland's Wife

Colombo, *Mysterious Canada*.

10. The *Fairie Queene*

Colombo, *Mysterious Canada*.

Roland H. Sherwood, *Maritime Mysteries: Haunting Tales from Atlantic Canada* (Windsor, N.S.: Lancelot Press, 1976).

11. The *Charles Haskell*

Colombo, *Mysterious Canada*.

12. Mr. Extry Man

Helen Creighton, *Bluenose Ghosts* (Toronto: Ryerson Press, 1957).

13. Joshua Slocum's Ghost
John Robert Colombo, *Extraordinary Experiences: Personal Accounts of the Paranormal in Canada* (Toronto: Hounslow Press, 1989).

14. The Codfish Man
Colombo, *Mysterious Canada.*

15. The Colonel's Ghost
Colombo, *Mysterious Canada.*

16. The Wynyard Apparition
Raymond Lamont Brown, *A Casebook of Military Mystery* (Cambridge: Stephens, 1974).
Edgar A. Collard, *Canadian Yesterdays* (Toronto: Longman's, Green, 1955).
John Robert Colombo, *Dark Visions: Personal Accounts of the Mysterious in Canada* (Toronto: Hounslow Press, 1992).
____, *Mysterious Canada.*
A. Patchett Martin, *Life and Letters of the Right Honourable Robert Lowe, Viscount Sherbrooke, G.C.B., D.C.L., Etc., With a Memoir of Sir John Coape Sherbrooke, G.C.B., Sometime Governor-General of Canada* (1893).
Seymour Phelps, "Walk around Town! O," *St. Catharines Journal,* August 1856. Reprinted in *St. Catharines A to Z* (St. Catharines, Ont.: St. Catharines and Lincoln Historical Society, 1967).

17. The Great Amherst Mystery
Anonymous, "The Amherst 'Mystery' at Moncton – Esther Cox Interviewed – The Spirit Disturbs a Church," *Daily Sun* (Saint John, N.B.), 23 June 1879.
Colombo, *Mysterious Canada.*

18. The Fire-Spook of Caledonia Mills
Colombo, *Dark Visions.*
____, *Mysterious Canada.*
N. Carroll Macintyre, *The Fire-Spook of Caledonia Mills* (Antigonish, N.S.: Sundown Publications, 1985).

19. The Little Man Who Wasn't There
Franklin P. Adams, *Innocent Merriment: An Anthology of Light Verse* (New York: Whittlesey House, 1942).
Colombo, *Mysterious Canada.*

20. The Phantom Train of Bras d'Or
Colombo, *Mysterious Canada*.
Mary L. Fraser, *The Folklore of Nova Scotia* (Toronto: Catholic Truth Society, 1932).

21. Haliburton House
Colombo, *Mysterious Canada*.

22. Hopper's Headstone
Colombo, *Mysterious Canada*.

23. The Dungarvon Whooper
Colombo, *Mysterious Canada*.

24. "52 North by 21 West"
Colombo, *Mysterious Canada*.
Edith Fowke, Unpublished research.

25. The Female Phantom of Gagetown
Colombo, *Mysterious Canada*.

26. Christ Church Ghost
Colombo, *Mysterious Canada*.

27. The Rowing Man
Colombo, *Mysterious Canada*.

28. Vision of a Newly Dead Friend
Colombo, *Mysterious Canada*.

29. The Little Man
Colombo, *Mysterious Canada*.

30. The Prophet's Room
Colombo, *Mysterious Canada*.

31. The UPEI Haunting
David K. MacKinnon, "Ghost Story of the Day," e-mail, 30 November 1997.

Quebec

32. The Talking Head
Colombo, *Mysterious Canada.*

33. The Quebec Werewolf
Colombo, *Mysterious Canada.*

34. The Hudson Poltergeist
Anonymous, "Mysterious Manifestations," *Daily Colonist* (Victoria, B.C.), 1 October
    1880.

35. Another Hudson Poltergeist
Anonymous, "Strange Doings," *Star* (Montreal, Que.), 25 May 1881.
Anonymous, "The St. Hubert Manifestations," *Star* (Montreal, Que.), 26 May 1881.
Anonymous, "The St. Hubert Mystery," *Star* (Montreal, Que.), 27 May 1881.
Anonymous, "The Spirits at St. Hubert," *Star* (Montreal, Que.), 28 May 1881.

36. The Walling-in of Peggy Green
Colombo, *Mysterious Canada.*

37. The Dagg Poltergeist
John Robert Colombo, *Ghost Stories of Ontario* (Toronto: Hounslow Press, 1995).
_____, *Mysterious Canada.*

38. Dr. Brunelle's Crisis Apparition
John Robert Colombo, *Marvellous Stories: Strange Events and Experiences from Canada's
    Past* (Toronto: Colombo & Company, 1998).

39. A Singular Case
Colombo, *Extraordinary Experiences.*
Sir Arthur Conan Doyle, *Our Second American Adventure* (Boston: Little, Brown, 1924).

40. Stalked by a Ghost
Anonymous, Article, *Evening Citizen* (Ottawa, Ont.), 23 November 1934.
John Robert Colombo, *Ghosts Galore! Personal Accounts of Hauntings in Canada*
    (Toronto: Colombo & Company, 1994).
Joan Finnigan, *Tell Me Another Story* (Toronto: McGraw-Hill Ryerson, 1988).

41. The Haunting of Willow Place Inn

Colombo, *Mysterious Canada.*

42. La Vieille Chapelle Ramsay

John Robert Colombo, Overnight visit and interview with Regina Makuch, La Vieille
Chapelle Ramsay, Chemin des Pères, Magog, Que., 14 July 1995.

Ontario

43. The Baldoon Mystery

Colombo, *Ghost Stories of Ontario.*

Neil T. McDonald, *The Baldoon Mysteries: A Weird Tale of the Early Scotch Settlers of
Baldoon* (Wallaceburg, Ont.: News Office, 1910).

44. Old McAfee

Colombo, *Mysterious Canada.*

45. The Eldon House Ghost

Colombo, *Mysterious Canada.*

46. Welsh Lullabies

Colombo, *Mysterious Canada.*

Paul Gosen, Correspondence, 12 December 1998.

47. Tom Thomson's Ghost

Colombo, *Mysterious Canada.*

48. The Vision of Old Walt

John Robert Colombo, *Mysterious Encounters: Personal Accounts of the Supernatural in
Canada* (Toronto: Hounslow Press, 1990).

Walter Franklin Prince, *Noted Witnesses for Psychic Occurrences* (Boston: Boston Society
for Psychic Research, 1928; New York: University Books, 1963).

49. Ambrose Small, Missing Man

Colombo, *Mysterious Canada.*

50. An Early Morning Visitor

John Robert Colombo, *Mackenzie King's Ghost and Other Personal Accounts of Canadian*

Hauntings (Toronto: Hounslow Press, 1991).

51. The Ghost of St. Columbkill's
Colombo, *Mysterious Canada.*

52. The Vision of the Chapel
Colombo, *Mackenzie King's Ghost.*
____, *Mysterious Canada.*

53. Mackenzie King's Ghost
Colombo, *Mackenzie King's Ghost.*
Percy J. Philip, "I Talked with Mackenzie King's Ghost," *Fate Magazine*, December 1955.
____, "My Conversation with Mackenzie King's Ghost," *Liberty*, January 1955.

54. The Haunting of Mackenzie House
Colombo, *Mackenzie King's Ghost.*

55. The Haunted Bookshop
Colombo, *Mysterious Canada.*

56. Elizabeth the Ghost
Colombo, *Mysterious Canada.*

57. The Haunting of Glanmore
John Robert Colombo, Visit to Glanmore, 24 September 1994; brochure titled *Glanmore!* (Hastings County Museum, n.d.); correspondence with Rona Rustige, curator/manager of Glanmore, 7 October 1994; conversations with former occupants Mrs. Anne Faulkner (15 October 1994) and Mrs. Philippa Faulkner (17 October 1994), now residents of Toronto.

58. The Screaming Tunnel
Colombo, *Mysterious Canada.*
Fred Habermehl, Correspondence, 19 April 1996.

59. The Bilotti House
Colombo, *Mysterious Canada.*

60. The Beautiful Lady in White

John Robert Colombo, *Haunted Toronto* (Toronto: Hounslow Press, 1996).

61. The Ghost of the Alex

Colombo, *Haunted Toronto*.

Michael Posner, "Who's That Treading the Boards?" *Globe and Mail*, 3 January 1998.

62. The Gibson-Atwood Ghost

Colombo, *Mysterious Canada*.

_____, *Extraordinary Experiences*.

63. A Very Strange Experience

Colombo, *Mackenzie King's Ghost*.

64. The Sticky Man

Colombo, *Mackenzie King's Ghost*.

65. The Vision of a Crime

Colombo, *Extraordinary Experiences*.

66. "Betty Louty"

Colombo, *Mysterious Encounters*.

67. Apparition of a Cat

Colombo, *Mysterious Encounters*.

68. Hunting Henry's Ghost

Colombo, *Ghost Stories of Ontario*.

69. The Most Beautiful Woman in the World

Colombo, *Ghost Stories of Ontario*.

70. Short Circuit

Colombo, *Ghost Stories of Ontario*.

Prairies

71. The White Horse
Colombo, *Mysterious Canada.*

72. Spirit of White Eagle
Colombo, *Mysterious Canada.*
John H. Hutton, *Gazette* (Montreal, Que.), 30 January 1934.

73. Who Calls?
Colombo, *Mysterious Canada.*

74. The Vanishing Village
Colombo, *Mysterious Canada.*
Sir Cecil Edward Denny, *The Riders of the Plains: A Reminiscence of the Early and Exciting Days of the North-west* (Calgary: The Herald, 1905).

75. Frog Lake Vision
Colombo, *Dark Visions.*
_____, *Mysterious Canada.*

76. The Travelling Ghost
Magnus Einarsson, *Icelandic-Canadian Oral Narratives,* Mercury Series, Canadian Centre for Folk Culture Studies, no. 63 (Ottawa: Canadian Museum of Civilization, 1991).

77. The Haunted House
Colombo, *Extraordinary Experiences.*
_____, *Mysterious Canada.*

78. The Haunted Duplex
John Robert Colombo, Unpublished files, correspondence with Elizabeth Vaadeland, Prince Albert, Sask., 17 March 1988.

79. The Ghost Train
Colombo, *Mysterious Canada.*
Ted Ferguson, *Sentimental Journey: An Oral History of Train Travel in Canada* (Toronto: Doubleday Canada, 1985).

80. The Lost Room
Colombo, *Mysterious Canada.*

81. The Ghost of Deane House
Colombo, *Mysterious Canada.*

82. Capitol Hill House
Colombo, *Mysterious Canada.*

83. Canmore Opera House Ghost
Colombo, *Mysterious Canada.*

84. Ghosts of Banff and Lake Louise
Colombo, *Mysterious Canada.*
Wayne MacDonald, *Calgary Albertan,* 3 February 1962.

West Coast

85. The Ghost Photograph
Colombo, *Mysterious Canada.*

86. The Headless Brakeman
Colombo, *Mysterious Canada.*
Ferguson, *Sentimental Journey.*

87. The Chilliwack Poltergeist
Colombo, *Mysterious Canada.*
R.S. Lambert, *Exploring the Supernatural in Canada: The Weird in Canadian Folklore* (Toronto: McClelland & Stewart, 1955).

88. The Spirit of the Hanging Judge
Colombo, *Mysterious Canada.*
_____, *Mysterious Encounters.*

89. Pursuit by Lightning
Albert A. Brandt, "Lightning to the End," *Fate Magazine,* April-May 1952.
Colombo, *Mysterious Canada.*

90. The Oak Bay Hauntings

Anonymous, "Century-Old Ghost Haunts Ex-Tod House at Oak Bay," *Vancouver Sun*, 13 February 1950.

Anonymous, "Old Victoria Mansion's Famous Ghost Stilled," *Calgary Herald*, 17 May 1952.

Fred Curtin, "Ghosts Back at Old Haunts," *Vancouver Province*, 9 April 1964.

Robin Skelton and Jean Kozocari, *A Gathering of Ghosts* (Saskatoon: Western Producer Prairie Books, 1989).

91. The Case of the Snoring Ghost

Colombo, *Mackenzie King's Ghost.*

Margery Wighton, "The Case of the Haunted House and Snoring Ghost," *Vancouver Sun*, 27 December 1952.

92. See the Dancing Indians

Jack Scott, "The Night I Began to Believe in Ghosts," *Vancouver Sun*, 28 August 1971; reprinted in *Great Scott!: A Collection of the Best Newspaper Columns* (Victoria: Sono Nis Press, 1985).

93. A Lady in the House

Colombo, *Extraordinary Experiences.*

94. The Chinese Ghost

Allan Blue, "What the Customers Saw," *Midtown Voice* (Toronto, Ont.), October 1991.

Colombo, *Ghosts Galore!*

95. The "Twilight Zone" Truck Stop

Colombo, *Mysterious Encounters.*

The North

96. Mackenzie River Ghost

Colombo, *Dark Visions.*

Roderick MacFarlane, "Ghost Story" (1883), *The Beaver*, December 1986-January 1987.

97. Spirit Rapping in the Far North

Anonymous, "Spirit Rapping in the Far North," *The Nor'-Wester* (Winnipeg and Red River Settlement), 1 December 1866.

Colombo, *Marvellous Stories.*

98. The Frozen City of the Yukon

Alexander Badlam, *The Wonders of Alaska* (San Francisco: Bancroft Company, 1890). Colombo, *Dark Visions.*

99. Ghost Ship of the Arctic Sea

Vincent Gaddis, *Invisible Horizons: Mysteries of the Sea* (Philadelphia: Chilton Books, 1965).

100. The Village of the Dead

Colombo, *Mysterious Canada.*

Frank Edwards, *Stranger than Science* (New York: Lyle Stuart, 1959).

Emmett E. Kelleher, "Tribe Lost in Barrens of North," *Herald* (Halifax, N.S.), 29 November 1930.

Dwight Whalen, "Vanished Village Revisited," *Fate Magazine*, November 1976.

Section Two

Barton, Winifred G. *Psychic Phenomena in Canada.* Ottawa: PSI-Science Productions, c. 1968.

Belyk, Robert C. *Ghosts: True Stories from British Columbia.* Ganges, B.C.: Horsdal & Schubart Publishers, 1990.

_____. *Ghosts II: More True Stories from B.C.* Ganges, B.C.: Horsdal & Schubart Publishers, 1997.

Boyle, Terry. *Haunted Ontario.* Toronto: Polar Bear Press, 1998.

Christensen, Jo-Anne. *Ghost Stories of British Columbia.* Toronto: Hounslow Press, 1996.

_____. *Ghost Stories of Saskatchewan.* Toronto: Hounslow Press, 1995.

Clery Val. *Ghost Stories of Canada.* Toronto: Hounslow Press, 1985.

Colombo, John Robert. *Close Encounters of the Canadian Kind.* Toronto: Colombo & Company, 1994.

_____. *Closer than You Think: Personal Accounts of the Unusual in Canada.* Toronto: Colombo & Company, 1998.

_____. *Colombo's Book of Marvels.* Toronto: NC Press, 1979.

_____. *Dark Visions: Personal Accounts of the Mysterious in Canada.* Toronto: Hounslow Press, 1992.

_____. *Extraordinary Experiences: Personal Accounts of the Paranormal in Canada.* Toronto: Hounslow Press, 1989.

_____. *Ghost Stories of Ontario.* Toronto: Hounslow Press, 1995.

_____. *Ghosts Galore! Personal Accounts of Hauntings in Canada.* Toronto: Colombo & Company, 1994.

_____. *Ghosts in Our Past: 60 True Ghost Stories from 19th-Century Canadian Newspapers.* Toronto: Colombo & Company, 2000.

_____. *Haunted Toronto.* Toronto: Hounslow Press, 1996.

_____. *Mackenzie King's Ghost and Other Personal Accounts of Canadian Hauntings.* Toronto: Hounslow Press, 1991.

_____. *Marvellous Stories: Strange Events and Experiences from Canada's Past.* Toronto: Colombo & Company, 1998.

_____. *Mysteries of Ontario.* Toronto: Hounslow Press, 1999.

_____. *Mysterious Canada: Strange Sights, Extraordinary Events, and Peculiar Places.* Toronto: Doubleday Canada, 1988.

_____. *Mysterious Encounters: Personal Accounts of the Supernatural in Canada.* Toronto: Hounslow Press, 1990.

_____. *The Mystery of the Shaking Tent.* Toronto: Hounslow Press, 1993.

_____. *Singular Stories: Tales of Wonder from 19th-Century Canadian Newspapers.* Toronto: Colombo & Company, 1999.

_____. *Strange Stories: Weird and Wonderful Events and Experiences from Canada's Past.* Toronto: Colombo & Company, 1994.

_____. *Three Mysteries of Nova Scotia.* Toronto: Colombo & Company, 1999.

_____. *UFOs over Canada.* Toronto: Hounslow Press, 1991.

_____. *Weird Stories: From 19th-Century Canadian Newspapers.* Toronto: Colombo & Company, 2000.

_____. *Windigo: An Anthology of Fact and Fantastic Fiction.* Saskatoon: Western Producer Prairie Books, 1992.

Creighton, Helen. *Bluenose Ghosts.* Toronto: Ryerson Press, 1957.

_____. *Folklore of Lunenburg County, Nova Scotia.* Toronto: McGraw-Hill Ryerson, 1976.

Fowke, Edith. *Folklore of Canada.* Toronto: McClelland & Stewart, 1976.

_____. *Folktales of French Canada.* Toronto: NC Press, 1981.

_____. *Legends Told in Canada.* Toronto: Royal Ontario Museum, 1994.

_____. *Tales Told in Canada.* Toronto: Doubleday Canada, 1986.

Hervey, Sheila. *Canada Ghost to Ghost.* Toronto: Stoddart/General, 1996.

_____. *Some Canadian Ghosts.* Toronto: Pocket Books/Simon & Schuster of Canada, 1973.

Lambert, R.S. *Exploring the Supernatural: The Weird in Canadian Folklore.* Toronto: McClelland & Stewart, 1955.

Mady, Najla. *Boo!! Ghosts I Have(n't) Loved.* Toronto: NC Press, 1993.

_____. *Simply Psychic.* St. Catharines, Ont.: The Author, 1983.

Owen, A.R.G. *Psychic Mysteries of Canada: Discoveries from the Maritime Provinces and Beyond.* Toronto: Harper & Row, 1975.

Owen, Iris M., with Margaret Sparrow. *Conjuring Up Philip: An Adventure in Psychokinesis.* Toronto: Fitzhenry & Whiteside, 1976.

Rutkowski, Chris A. *Abductions & Aliens: What's Really Going On?* Toronto: Hounslow Press, 1999.

_____. *Mysterious Manitoba.* Winnipeg: UFOROM, 1997.

_____. *Unnatural History: True Manitoba Mysteries.* Winnipeg: Chameleon Publishers, 1993.

Skelton, Robin, and Jean Kozocari. *A Gathering of Ghosts: Hauntings and Exorcisms from the Personal Casebook of Robin Skelton and Jean Kozocari.* Saskatoon: Western Producer Prairie Books, 1989.

Smith, Barbara. *Ghost Stories of Alberta.* Toronto: Hounslow Press, 1993.

_____. *Ghost Stories of Manitoba.* Edmonton: Lone Pine Publishing, 1998.

_____. *More Ghost Stories of Alberta.* Edmonton: Lone Pine Publishing, 1998.

_____. *Ontario Ghost Stories.* Edmonton: Lone Pine Publishing, 1998.

Sonin, Eileen. *ESPecially Ghosts: Some True Experiences of the Supernatural in North America.* Toronto: Clarke, Irwin, 1970; reissued as *More Canadian Ghosts.* Markham, Ont.: Pocket Books, 1974.

_____. *Ghosts I Have Known: The Psychic Experiences of a Natural Medium.* Toronto: Clarke, Irwin, 1968.

Watson, Julie V. *Ghost Stories and Legends of Prince Edward Island.* Toronto: Hounslow Press, 1988.

Postface

Have you enjoyed reading these accounts of strange events and eerie experiences? Have you experiences of your own you wish to relate?

I continue to collect accounts of such mysteries, and I encourage readers who have had events or experiences of a supernatural or para-psychological nature to share them with me and with my future readers.

Write to me care of the publisher:

Editorial Department
Hounslow Press
The Dundurn Group
8 Market St., Suite 200
Toronto, ON M5E 1M6
Canada

Or contact me directly by e-mail or through my homepage:

« *jrc@inforamp.net* »
« *http://www.inforamp.net/~jrc* »